SPIRIT OF THE GRASSROOTS PEOPLE

SPIRIT OF THE GRASSROOTS PEOPLE

Seeking Justice for Indigenous Survivors of
Canada's Colonial Education System

RAYMOND MASON

Edited by Jackson Pind and Theodore Michael Christou

McGill-Queen's University Press
Montreal & Kingston · London · Chicago

© McGill-Queen's University Press 2020

ISBN 978-0-2280-0351-9 (cloth)
ISBN 978-0-2280-0485-1 (ePDF)
ISBN 978-0-2280-0486-8 (ePUB)

Legal deposit fourth quarter 2020
Bibliothèque nationale du Québec

Printed in Canada on acid-free paper that is 100% ancient forest free
(100% post-consumer recycled), processed chlorine free

This book has been published with the help of a grant from the Canadian
Federation for the Humanities and Social Sciences, through the Awards to
Scholarly Publications Program, using funds provided by the Social Sciences
and Humanities Research Council of Canada.

We acknowledge the support of the Canada Council for the Arts.

Nous remercions le Conseil des arts du Canada de son soutien.

Library and Archives Canada Cataloguing in Publication

Title: Spirit of the grassroots people : seeking justice for indigenous survivors
    of Canada's colonial education system / Raymond Mason ; edited by Jackson
    Pind and Theodore Michael Christou.
Names: Mason, Raymond, 1946– author. | Pind, Jackson, 1993– editor. |
    Christou, Theodore Michael, editor.
Description: Includes bibliographical references and index.
Identifiers: Canadiana (print) 20200266322 | Canadiana (ebook) 20200266543 |
    ISBN 9780228003519 (cloth) | ISBN 9780228004851 (ePDF) | ISBN
    9780228004868 (ePUB)
Subjects: LCSH: Mason, Raymond, 1946– | LCSH: Ojibwa Indians—Manitoba—
    Biography. | LCSH: Adult child abuse victims—Manitoba—Biography. |
    CSH: Indians of North America—Canada—Residential schools. | LCGFT:
    Autobiographies.
Classification: LCC E99.C6 M36 2020 | DDC 371.829/97071—dc23

Set in 10/14 Radiata, Opinion Pro Light, and Cyntho Pro
Book design & typesetting by Garet Markvoort, zijn digital

CONTENTS

PREFACE: TWO-EYED SEEING AND STORYTELLING

This is Raymond Mason's story. Raymond, an Elder from the Peguis First Nation, is a Survivor of the Indian residential schools and an advocate for fellow Survivors. He has been a boxer, a military private, an entrepreneur, a husband, a father, a friend, a sibling, a son. Like each of us, Raymond has lived multiple lives and various existences. Raymond's story touches on each of these. His story is a link to that of other residential school Survivors and it is inimitably unique.

What you encounter here is presented in a manner that limits our interference in the story. We have curated the story. We have never told it. We are allies and friends; editors and transcribers; curators.

You may read this at multiple levels. If you do not wish to encounter us at all, forsake the remainder of this preface, the afterword, and the notes. These all exist because Raymond has brought them into existence by weaving us into his story in a curatorial, editorial role. We are linked to the story as stagehands in a play, except that we have moved punctuation rather than props.

Raymond decided that his story should reflect the premises of two-eyed seeing, wherein both Indigenous and Western ways of telling exist, intertwined, offering support. The oral history tells Raymond's experience. His story is truth. We have transcribed this and added notes that help to contextualize the story; we are supplementing, rather than supporting, Raymond's story.

Shawn Wilson's *Research Is Ceremony* notes, "Indigenous people in Canada recognize that it is important for storytellers to impart their own life and experience in to the telling. They also recognize that listeners will filter the story being told through their own experience and thus adapt the information to make it relevant and specific to their life. When listeners know where the storyteller is coming from and how the story fits into the storyteller's life, it makes the absorption of the knowledge that much easier."[1]

As researchers situated in the territory of the Haudenosaunee and the Anishinaabe at Queen's University, we engage in a method of storytelling that will allow you to hear Raymond's story even as we help to underline the broader historical narrative. Ray's story is like others' stories and part of the fabric of a larger history, and yet it is entirely unique and sufficient in its own right.

Theodore Michael Christou and Jackson Pind, 2020

CHRONOLOGY OF RAYMOND MASON'S LIFE

1946   Born on Matheson Island, Manitoba
1948   Ninette Sanatorium for tuberculosis treatment
1952   Peguis Day School #3 (failed grade one, moved to
        residential school)
1953   Sent to Birtle Residential School (seven years old)
1958   Sent to Portage la Prairie Residential School (twelve years old)
1962   Mother passed away (Katherine Mason, née Prince)
1963   Sent to Dauphin-Mackay Residential School (seventeen
        years old)
1964   Released from school, moved to Thompson, Manitoba
1968   Joined Armed Forces of Canada
1970   Moved to Aunt Nora's in Winnipeg to work on business degree
1975   Moved to Swan Lake First Nation as director of operations
1983   Moved to Edmonton, sought treatment for addictions
1986   Started meeting with other survivors in Winnipeg at St Regis
        Hotel to form the Manitoba Indian Residential School
        Survivors group
1995   Moved back to home community of Peguis First Nation and
        founded janitorial business
2000   Married Rhoda Mae Forster at Peguis First Nation
2003   Spirit Wind name adopted, formal organization started with
        the support of Manitoba Chiefs
2005   Testified in the House of Commons at the Aboriginal Standing
        Committee, provided support to 2005 Baxter National
        Class Action, which became 2006 Indian Residential School
        Settlement Agreement
2009   Day School Class Action launched with help of lawyer
        Joan Jack
2009–18 Continued activism for day school survivors, settled lawsuit
        while in attendance at House of Commons, 6 December 2018

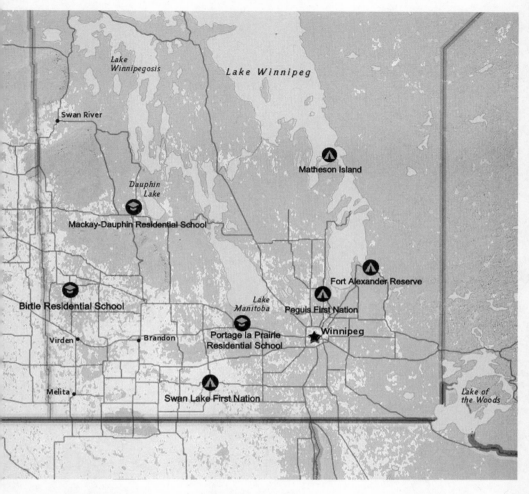

Map of southern Manitoba showing points of interest in Raymond Mason's life. Created by Jackson Pind with ArcGIS software.

SPIRIT OF THE GRASSROOTS PEOPLE

1 INTRODUCTION: THE BEGINNING

Do I tell the truth and disturb the contentment and feelings of the people who think that they did their best for the Survivors of the Indian residential schools?

Do I tell Canada and those people about the many disappointments, the hard work behind the scenes that was never revealed? Do I tell them that our efforts went unnoticed and that people were ungrateful? And that we were never given any credit for our hard work and lobbying for so many Survivors, for years before the political leadership of the Assembly of First Nations signed an agreement that excluded many of us Survivors.

Will Canada care about Spirit Wind, a small grassroots organization that came out of the woodwork, and that we are the ones who are still working in the trenches?

I want to tell you about our efforts, that it was us who played a key role in the coming to fruition of the Indian Residential School Settlement Agreement of Canada (IRSSA) and just recently the Day School Class Action. We were among the very first to bring forward the idea of lawsuits for the wrongdoings and the idea that Canada owed us for what happened to us in the colonial system. We were the very first people to talk about this topic, long before any Native organization or persons ever got involved to help bring about the agreement.

I will tell the world, and Canada, that we at Spirit Wind are the advocates and lobbyists for the grassroots people, the Survivors of the colonial education systems of Canada. I would like to dedicate this book to those Survivors who did not live to see the day when agreements came to pass or true justice. In the memory of those who did not live to see this day, may their spirits be at peace. Our efforts did not end with the IRSSA. Spirit Wind continues to fight for the recognition of Survivors from all schools not included in the IRSSA, including the Indian day school Survivors.

In this book I will attempt to summarize, paraphrase, and provide an insight into what really happened, behind the scenes, to bring the Indian Residential School Settlement Agreement of Canada to fruition. As we know, there were quite a number of people who played a role during the early, developmental period of the eventual IRSS Agreement between the late 1980s and 2005. This needs to be recognized and considered because a lot of effort and lobbying happened behind the scenes that went unnoticed by the people who received all the accolades for something that they really did not do.

There were other people who did their share of very important work as well. We at Spirit Wind played a significant role in bringing about the agreement. We want our accolades, too, as it is only fair that we receive them. In this book, I hope to clarify why we are adamant about receiving credit and that people will learn about our efforts and the contributions of survivors.

I write and speak about my life without prejudice because my memory may play some tricks on me. I may say some things or describe events in a manner that is not liked or accepted universally, but these words represent the truth to the best of my knowledge. I tell this story truthfully. I apologize if I offend anyone for speaking these truths. I will give credit where credit is due, even though we never got the credit that we should have received. I will not hide my anger, but I will never give up until we, Spirit Wind, the representatives of the Grassroots Peoples, get what we deserve for all our lobbying, our hard work, and our efforts, and that is respect and appreciation.

You will note that in my book, I include a short biography of myself during my early years, which is also the story of my day school and residential school experience of twelve years in Birtle Indian Residential School, Portage la Prairie Indian Residential School, and Dauphin Mackay Indian Residential School, all in Manitoba. The reason I share this history – my story, my experiences in these schools – is to show that I write about matters I experienced first-hand. This book has an appendix composed of my personal documents relating to events in my life. It offers evidence of my life story and of Spirit Wind's history. I also include anecdotes from others who were with me when they shared their testimonies and experiences before the Aboriginal Standing Committee in the House of Commons in Ottawa.

My story needs to be told for a number of reasons, ranging from educational purposes to the historical need to expose the truth about how these multibillion-dollar agreements came into existence. Nobody knows what took place behind the scenes. Spirit Wind and I have worked very hard over the years lobbying and pressing to make Canada admit that it harmed us and did wrong by us. The Government of Canada stymied us repeatedly, delaying our efforts in various ways. We were snubbed by various officials, even when we helped our lawyers win the court case that led to the eventual settlement agreement, which Spirit Wind and I signed in 2005.

Spirit Wind worked on a voluntary basis, never received any acknowledgment, and was quickly forgotten once the court case was won. I hope this book will bring more awareness about all the work that we accomplished, but also that it will help advocates and Survivors heal.[1] I seek to offer a fuller explanation of what it took to win the Indian Residential School Settlement Agreement.[2] Spirit Wind's mission statement was simple, and we were always guided by this statement (Appendix D):

Whereas; Spirit Wind is a grassroots network that unites into one voice and cause all Aboriginal Survivors who attended Indian Residential Schools throughout Manitoba and Canada.

Whereas; the Indian Residential School System operated by the Government of Canada and the Churches of Canada inflicted and implemented severe physical, sexual, emotional, psychological abuse, as well as a deliberate policy of cultural genocide, on generations of First Nations children across Manitoba and Canada.

Whereas; Spirit Wind is guided by the Spirit and provides Aboriginal People the strength, courage, and conviction to fight for dignity, respect, and fair, just, and expedient consideration and compensation from the Government of Canada and Churches for our pain and suffering.

Whereas; Spirit Wind is determined to gain justice and healing for all Residential School Survivors and families that have endured ongoing pain and suffering as a legacy of the Residential School System.

Whereas; Spirit Wind is on a journey to educate the public, media, and politicians on the destructive effects and legacy of abuse and cultural genocide inflicted on First Nations people throughout Canada.

Whereas; the Government of Canada must recognize that everyone who attended an Indian Residential School is entitled to and will receive fair and just individual compensation for emotional, psychological abuse and cultural and language genocide as well as physical and sexual abuse.

Be it Resolved; Spirit Wind will continue to grow across Canada and unite and advocate for all Residential School Survivors until justice and fairness are achieved as guided by our Spirit.[3]

I would like to thank all the people who supported me in my efforts to make my book happen, including Jackson Pind, Dr Theodore Michael Christou, Dr Jennifer Davis, Jill McConkey, and Michelle Leitz, for helping edit my story and providing advice on writing this type of work. I am also deeply indebted to the friendship and guidance of our acquisition editor, Mark Abley, who believed in this project and worked tirelessly to bring it to fruition. His efforts to work with Indigenous people in a reconciliatory manner, alongside expert advice in navigating the academic publishing world, have been an essential part in creating this story. I would also like to thank the staff at McGill-Queen's University Press for providing such helpful advice every step of the process. In particular, I am especially grateful for the work of our copyeditor, Kate Merriman, for her meticulous edit of the final version. I would also like to thank Amanda Marsh for her help in improving the quality of the images used in the book, and Ruth Pincoe for her support of this project and the index. Finally, I would not have been able to travel throughout Canada spreading this message without the help of Peguis First Nation and my chief, Glenn Hudson. I give thanks to the many people who told me that my story was worthwhile and would now provide others with the opportunity to read about the history of the IRSS Agreement.

I would like to acknowledge and thank all the former national Indian Residential School Survivors Society board members and their staff who worked along with Spirit Wind to achieve success for the Indian residential school Survivors of Canada and day school Survivors.

I would also wish to thank "all our relations" for the love, caring, sharing, and standing up to this cause. Thank you to my family for standing by me and believing in me, especially my wife Rhoda and her children.

Raymond Mason, 2020

2 CATCHING UP WITH MYSELF

I would like to tell my story of how the Indian Residential Schools Settlement Agreement (IRSSA) came about. This story includes my involvement in the IRSSA process and how I helped bring it to fruition. I want the people, and the politicians, both Canadian and political representatives of First Nations people, to know how difficult it was to gain this settlement, including all the highs and lows we experienced during the stages of the development. I would like the people to learn the full history of what it took to develop the IRSSA. It did not happen overnight. It took many, many years of hard, exhausting work. I feel that our story has to be heard and to be respected.

The story begins with me and with my former schoolmates having hundreds of cups of coffee at the St Regis Hotel restaurant in Winnipeg, Manitoba, from about 1986 until 1997.[1] We would talk and reminisce about our time in the residential schools. We would laugh and talk about all of the good things and the bad things we experienced in those days. Sometimes our discussions would become very emotional and sad when we talked about the lonely and the hard times.

We talked about how scared we had been, and how worried about the unknown, not certain about what could happen to us. We talked about the hard work we had to do in the school. We talked about all the fighting amongst ourselves, and about the sexual abuse. We talked about how we did not know how to deal with the fact that we were sexually abused. We talked about how we were scared and embarrassed to tell anyone for fear of being ridiculed and laughed at.

Even though we discussed it frequently at our gatherings, it really never registered what really happened to us. But I did notice how we seemed to be different and distant from our sisters and brothers who were fortunate enough not to go to a residential school. As I later found out, some of my friends did not go to the IRS schools because our parents hid them whenever the Indian agent came around to pick them up. My wife, Rhoda, is one of those children. Rhoda never attended residential schools despite coming from the same reserve as me, and she was able to lead a healthy life full of love. I had always wondered why some Indigenous people were in such dire straits while others were able to adapt and fit into new ways of life.

Then one day at the St Regis, I spoke about how Canada apologized to the Japanese Canadians in 1988 for being interned during the Second World War. I had heard on the news that Japanese Canadians had won their lawsuit against the government and they would have to provide compensation with the apology.[2] At the time, Prime Minister Brian Mulroney said compensation was morally and ethically the right thing to do. I soon realized that if Canada can compensate Japanese Canadians for forcing them into the camps, they should compensate us for crimes we had experienced in the residential schools.[3]

We thought that as Japanese Canadians were interned in camps during the Second World War period and received a significant settlement for being forcibly contained, Canada had also committed the same sorts of crimes against Indigenous Canadians. We wanted Canada to follow the same principle and have the federal government deal with the residential school issues. We said that Canada should compensate us for sticking us in schools far from home and for the way we were mistreated and horribly abused.

That is when we, five former Dauphin Residential School classmates, first started to talk about going after Canada for compensation for what they had put us through. We felt that we were owed something, but we were not sure what amount it should be. We talked about an apology, financial compensation, and how to educate the rest of Canada (people outside "Indian" country) about what they did to us and how the Canadian government tried to take the "Indian out of the child"[4] – in our words, "assimilation."[5]

We want the people of Canada to know what the colonial system did with its residential schools and institutions, the dysfunctional impact it had on our people, our communities, and our culture. We want the people of Canada to know that today, if a child is taken from his or her family (mother and father), community, and culture, this is "child abduction" and cultural genocide.[6] We want the people to know that Canada never succeeded in their efforts to "take the Indian out of the child," but efforts to do so did much severe damage to our people. Many of us became alcoholics, frustrated, confused, and very angry at the world. We were not able to cope with the poverty, substance abuse, and the breakdown of our sacred family bonds, which had held us together as nations and communities for thousands of years.

For many years, people have wondered why jails and prisons have such a high representation of Indigenous inmates while Indigenous people are such a small percent of the overall population.[7] This overrepresentation should not be surprising, considering the lasting effects of the residential school system. It has been found that many Indigenous people in prison suffer from generational trauma caused by experiences at the residential schools, even to this day.[8] I also would end up in jail throughout my life for a variety of reasons as I struggled to find meaning in a world that had separated me from my family for twelve long years beginning at the age of six.

Also, you can see much dysfunction in our communities because of economic instability and lack of resources. This leads to third-world levels of poverty and infrastructure.[9] There is not enough money to build the necessary components that make a community operate with few or no needs. For as long as I can remember, our communities have lacked basic financial resources and resources for quality living requirements. We continue to live with inadequate funding for our educational systems, housing, and wellness programs within our communities. These issues help perpetuate a cycle of abuse that has continued long after the first residential schools were illegally erected on our lands.[10]

These are some of the issues that gave us, who met at St Regis, the drive to act. I told my friends that we should organize ourselves so that we could be a recognized group. We developed a mission statement promising to lobby for justice, financial compensation, and an apology from Canada. I never dreamed that this idea would grow as fast as it did. At the time, we thought that we would do this just for ourselves. After a while, as we began to realize the magnitude of our project, I made a personal promise that I would never rest in peace until all Survivors in Canada got what they deserved: respect, justice, compensation, and an apology from the Government of Canada. I have received my apology from the Anglican Church for their "part in creating a legacy of trauma" but many other Survivors have not (Appendix A). This book will demonstrate how the spirit of the grassroots people came together in order to seek justice from Canada for their crimes.

As it turned out, Canada divided us into different Survivor categories: Indian residential school Survivors, day school Survivors, and other Survivors who were placed in the "unofficial" schools like Teulon Residential School in Manitoba.[11] All these Survivors deserve justice as well, not just those recognized in the official agreement. I suspect that these institutions were excluded from the agreement because Canada did not want to pay for all the abuses to our people, and classifying them into different categories would lessen their responsibilities. As Survivors, we do not see these arbitrary divisions, but rather support all efforts for former students of the colonial system to seek justice.

After meeting and talking about it for a few years, we decided to give ourselves a name to operate under: the "Manitoba Indian Residential School Movement." The five members (former school buddies) were as follows:

Russell Tobacco (deceased)
Hubert Kematch (deceased)
Danny Highway (lives in Winnipeg, Manitoba)
Clifford Kematch (missing)
Melvin Swan (joined us a little later on, lives in Winnipeg,
    Manitoba)
Myself, Ray Mason

We decided that we would "spread the word" across the country about what Canada did by sticking us in these residential schools, that it was wrong, and that the Government of Canada owed us something for the abuses that we suffered. We started to speak to our chiefs, grand chiefs, and our political organizations across Canada and to people that we knew who had gone to residential school.[12]

We found that "spreading the word" was a lot harder than we first thought, and the main reason for that was because none of us had the money to help pay the cost of travel and other expenses (e.g., phone calls). So, we did the best we could by word of mouth, on a voluntary basis. During my work and my travels, I would go to speak to our chiefs and ask them if they could help us, in any kind of manner, by lending us some office space. Our first major letdown was when a chief told me that I was "barking up the wrong tree" because suing Canada is like a "David and Goliath fight" and that I had very little chance of succeeding. Before I left his office, I turned to him and said, "Yes, I guess I agree with you about that David and Goliath fight, but don't forget who won that fight."[13]

We also knew we needed a lawyer, so we set out to hire one. Hiring a lawyer was a real big task because none of us had any money to pay a retainer fee. It took us four years, until 1990, to finally get a lawyer who was willing to "look into" our concerns and check things out. All other lawyers would put us through hoops, and we spent much time explaining why we wanted to sue Canada. It always ended up with them wanting a retainer fee of $40,000, some $60,000, others $80,000 to $100,000 before they would go any further.[14] This was money we never dreamed of ever having, so things would look very bleak at times. Finally, after many attempts and many years, we came across a gentleman, Mr Dennis Troniak, who was a lawyer and was willing to take on our case. Man, oh man, I cried with joy because I was beginning to get discouraged and didn't have much faith left, at that time.[15] He was the first lawyer to listen to my story intently and did not want a retainer fee. I later found out that he had a personal connection to the schools as his wife was Métis.[16]

About this time, I was beginning to get depressed about how slowly things were developing and the many letdowns we were experiencing. I always managed to pick myself up and call my colleagues and tell them we can't give up and that we must give each other encouragement to carry on our cause. I knew if I don't succeed, the Survivors won't succeed, and those people out there were depending on us.

3   MY EARLY YEARS

I was born to Katherine (née Prince) and Elijah Mason in 1946 on Matheson Island near the shores of Lake Winnipeg. My mother was born of the late Edith and Albert Edward Prince. My grandmother came from the Berens River First Nation area, near Berens River on the east side of Lake Winnipeg. Apparently, she was half Scottish, but I don't know which of her parents was Scottish. My grandfather on my mother's side was the grandson of the great Chief Peguis, who granted land and assistance to the Selkirk settlers at Red River.[1] He was born on and came from the old St Peter's Reserve, located north of Winnipeg in the area of St Andrews, Selkirk, and East Selkirk, Manitoba. St Peter's Reserve was once where all of our people lived and came from, before the relocation to Peguis First Nation.[2]

My father was from Fisher River Cree Nation, but he passed on before I got to know him. I was told that I was only two years old when he passed away because of the tuberculosis disease. I never remembered meeting my father as he died when I was so young; however, I have one story that was told to me growing up. I heard that he was a very hard worker and that when he first caught tuberculosis he thought he was getting lazy and tired for nothing and pushed himself until he died.[3] My parents had five children. I had one brother and three sisters:

Edith Mason
Stanley Mason
Nora Mason
Myself, Raymond Mason
Verna Ethal Mason

After my father passed on, my mother moved back to Peguis First Nation, then known as Peguis Reserve. Shortly after moving back, she met Ross Daniels. They married and gave me seven more siblings:

Clarence Daniels
Bernice Daniels
Marlene Joyce Daniels
Sharon Marie Daniels

Beverly Ann Daniels
Phyllis Faye Daniels
Darryl Ross Daniels

I grew up with my mother and my step-dad, Ross Daniels, for a short while. I learned later on in life that my older sisters, Edith and Nora, were being brought up by our grandparents (the Prince side) and that my older brother, Stanley, was being brought up by one of my uncles, Ed Prince, and his wife Edna, while Verna and I stayed with my mom. I did not realize that I had other sisters and a brother (on the Mason side) until I was eight years old. My family had now extended to nearly twelve and despite living in different areas, times were tough.[4]

I remember our home was made of logs (like a big log cabin), small, two floors high, the inside and outside walls chinked with moss and clay mud and whitewashed with a mixture of lime and wood fire ash. Every home on the reserve was made of the same materials and blended in with the snowy white winter months. We had to carry our drinking water from the river, cut firewood, and keep a fire on to stay warm and for cooking. Things were a lot different back then, as we didn't have electricity, radio, or television, and we mostly just focused on surviving.[5] My stepfather would work gathering "lent wood" of dried trees that they would sell on the road for other people's fires and he would hunt deer to help provide for the large family. Our only, and main, source of entertainment would come in the summer months as we would go swimming as a family after a long day in the prairie heat.

As it turns out, I was diagnosed with tuberculosis, TB as we knew it in those days, shortly after my father passed on.[6] At age two years old I was sent off to the Ninette Sanatorium near Brandon, Manitoba (a distance of 250 kilometres), for medical treatment. It is very difficult to remember this period of my life now, but I remember coming home after four years and my mother explaining that I was now six years old and have to go to the nearby school. I still have scars on my finger, foot, and back from tuberculosis, but the most lasting scar was that I could not speak English, and it was punishing all that time not being able to communicate with the nurses or any other classmates.[7]

I recall that I was the oldest child of the family, so I had to do most of the work around the house such as cutting wood, doing chores, and

Raymond's mother and younger siblings, pre-1950. Used with permission of Raymond Mason.

keeping up with housework. I remember going to the local day school (Peguis #3 School) to do my grade one at the age of six after returning from the sanatorium around 1952. My stepfather, Ross, was a very stern and strict sergeant-like person, but on the other hand he taught me how to be tough.[8] I respect that he brought me up the way he did as I learned early on how to defend myself. I failed grade one and to this day I will never forget it, because I had to go to the bush and pick out a red willow for my spanking because Ross was so disappointed that I had not done better.[9] He had attended residential schools so he believed that this was the proper manner to raise children.[10]

In the next year, I was still struggling to get caught up in English as the sanatorium let me speak in my traditional tongue. I was doing quite badly in school as a result, and I remember being about seven or eight years old when one morning, the Indian agent and a police officer came to the house to take me away to a residential school.[11] It was in the morning, as the bus to Winnipeg was waiting for me, and I remember my sisters, brother, and my mom crying out loud.[12] My stepfather was also putting up a big fuss about them coming to take me away.[13] During the commotion, my younger sister Verna ran off and hid in the bush so that she would not also be taken.[14] My mother hung on to me as long as she could, but the Indian agent told her that I would be better off and at a better place and that I would be well looked after and not to worry about me.[15]

There was a Grey Goose bus service from Peguis to Winnipeg then and they put me on board without even a change of clothes. I remember the Indian agent telling the bus driver to watch me very closely and not to let me out of his sight, and to see that I got on the bus to Birtle, Manitoba (Birtle is almost 400 kilometres from Peguis). I was alone and I didn't even have a clue where I was going. Or what was going on with me. I remember the bus driver telling me to sit right behind him so that he could keep a close eye on me.[16] We would drive for three hours and I would arrive in Winnipeg, Manitoba for the first time that I remembered.[17]

I had never been away from home before this, except to go to the local school (about half a mile) and to the sanatorium in Ninette, Manitoba, let alone a large city like Winnipeg. I had to sit in one place for hours on end to wait to be put on the bus to Birtle. I was so terrified, and did nothing but cry most of the time. I had to sit in this great big building with hundreds of people walking by me, looking at me as if I was a strange animal. It was a big place and I had never seen that much electricity before, but I was very hungry and too scared to ask for food or to use the washroom. I eventually peed on myself as I couldn't help it. I was too scared to even speak one word as I had already understood what happened if I spoke my language.[18]

Finally, one of the officials or someone came and gave me a sandwich, but it was just like feeding a dog. The bus depot officials made me sit in one place where they could keep a close eye on me. I was so damn scared I didn't even think about running away, because when I looked at all the tall buildings around me, I was petrified.[19] This was one of the first traumatic things that happened to me. When I think about it today, a dog gets treated better than I ever did. This was "child abduction." If it was a person and not a government taking me, they would be charged, and I don't see why these people that did this to me should be treated any differently.

Finally, after many horrific hours, I was put on a Grey Goose bus again, not knowing where the hell I was going. All I remember is that it was a long, long bus ride. Finally, when we arrived, it was totally dark at night. I was taken to the terminal officials and made to wait for someone to come

Birtle Residential School, 1931. Used with permission of Dr Gordon Goldsborough from his personal collection on residential schools.

to pick me up and to take me some place (as I later learned, it was the Birtle Indian Residential School).[20]

After I had waited for some time at the Birtle bus depot, two women came asking for me. Again, I was taken away in their vehicle, not knowing what was going to happen to me. It seemed like a very long ride, and they put me in the middle between them. I remember being stopped. We parked, I guess, and one of the women was commenting on how good looking and handsome I was. One of them started to push her fingers through my hair and started to "feel me up" between my legs. I had no clue what the hell she was doing to me. All I know is that I was scared and wanted to die. I didn't know what was going on. I thought that I was going to die right then and there. I was told not to mention a thing to anyone, or I would be in big trouble.

When we got to the school, I was taken to a big brick building. It was very dark. A man met us at the door and took me up about two or three flights of stairs, where I was given a bunk bed to sleep in. There was very little light. I was so tired I fell asleep instantly, despite all of my anxiety. After all of this, the next day I was sent to classes in another building of the compound.

(above) Aerial view of Birtle Residential School, n.d. Used with permission of Dr Gordon Goldsborough from his personal collection on residential schools.

(below) Birtle Residential School, n.d. Used with permission of Dr Gordon Goldsborough from his personal collection on residential schools.

I was provided with clothes and they told me that I would now be attending Birtle Residential School. We would typically wake up at sunrise and eat downstairs in the dining room and would later clean the floors before we were sent to classes.[21] When we got back from classes, we were all assigned different jobs in helping run the school. My job was cleaning and looking after the thirty to fifty pigs that were kept on the Birtle grounds.

The average nature of the days was surrounded by abuses at every turn, which really determined my schooling experience. Immediately upon arrival, I would begin to be sexually abused by other, bigger students and staffers, with continual strapping for speaking my native language. Since times were tough back home, I now didn't have to worry about food, although it seemed that there was never enough, and we had to work hard on the farms for what little food we did get.[22]

When I first arrived, an older man tried to sexually assault me after class, but I kicked him right in the chest. He got even more mad and made me clean the concrete steps outside of the school with a toothbrush. I later realized that this type of punishment was common for resisting abuse and everybody knew that when you were cleaning the steps you had just been a victim. The older kids would then poke fun at you because they also had been punished in the same way.[23]

Within the first few months another student and I decided that we wanted to run away from Birtle. We were always told if you follow the railway tracks, it would get you home. So, I just ran, and ran, and ran. My only goal was to make it back home. They caught me within the first day, but I never heard again from my friend who ran away on that day.

I was apprehended by two older students and a local Royal Canadian Mounted Police (RCMP) officer who helped the principal track me down. This would occur a few more times, but that first night of punishment may have been the worst. I was caught each time, and I was punished severely. I was used as an example to show the others that if you ever think of running away, this is what would happen to you.

I was tied to a bed in a star fashion, my clothes stripped off, and strapped until I would pass out. This happened in front of other children in my dormitory.[24] You could have heard a pin drop during the strapping, and I was strapped so long I didn't feel a thing, just warmth.[25] Today, I still carry some of those scars on my back and butt end.

Despite all of that, I would not give up. Sometimes I thought I might as well be dead than to have to live a life like this, in fear, anger, and to be abused worse than an animal. I guess you could say that I became a "problem" child, very hard to control and also very temperamental – a fly-off-the-handle type of child – a "savage," as they called us. The school had turned me into the very thing that the government saw in us, during their feeble attempts to "civilize" and educate us.

I cannot remember whether it was one or two years that I lasted in Birtle, but the weirdest thing of all took place in this institution. The whole time that I was there, I didn't know that my two oldest sisters, Edith and Nora, were in the same building as I was. A wall divided us so that we could not see or speak to each other. When I did see my sister Nora, at a Sunday church service, I spotted her on the "female side" of the aisle and I ran over to her, crying. I tried to hug her. I grabbed her and wouldn't let her go. She could not respond to me, because I was breaking a rule. We were not allowed to do what I was doing, trying to see and hug my sister.[26]

The male supervisors separated us, and again used me as an example: when you break this rule, this is what will happen to you. I had my pants taken off and I was strapped in front of every student. Again, I bled and passed out. Finally, the principal's wife had to stop them from strapping and hitting me before they killed me. This is some of the horrific torture and abuse that I endured while I was in the Birtle school. It is no wonder I personally held a grudge against this whole system.

Later, I was transferred to the Portage la Prairie Indian Residential School, around 1958. I think I was about twelve or thirteen years old but it is difficult to remember specific dates during this time of my life. I remember being a little older and a little bigger. In Birtle, I had learned to be a "scrapper," and when I came to Portage la Prairie, I was able to defend myself a lot easier.[27] Things were much different at Portage. We lived, slept, worked, and ate at the residence, and we were transported by bus to various schools in downtown Portage la Prairie. One school I attended was called the Fort la Reine School, and the other school that I went to, I can't remember. It was right in the middle of the town. I guess you could say this was our "integration period" with the non-Native students.[28]

This is when things got really ugly for me as more freedom was provided, but in restrictive avenues. When I attended classes in downtown Portage, the white boys would gang up on me and call me all sorts of

Portage la Prairie Residential School, n.d. Used with permission of Dr Gordon Goldsborough from his personal collection on residential schools.

names, such as "you dumb, no good, stinking Indian." About four or five of them would get me in a corner, kick me, spit on me, and laugh at me. This is because we used to have our hair cut funny looking and we had to wear old, ragged clothing from the schools. I had to quickly learn how to fight and to defend myself or be killed.[29]

I used to go tell our teacher. At first, she would scold them for what they were doing to me, but after that, it became "old hat news" to her and she ignored my pleas for help. I became a very good fighter and defended myself, and so they began to leave me alone. However, at the residence of Portage la Prairie IRS School, in the evenings when we were supposed to be doing our homework, the abuses would begin amongst ourselves. The bigger boys would beat us up and sexually abuse us during the nights when we were supposed to be sleeping.

I found myself always being lonely and wondering if I ever would be able to go home and live with my mother and the rest of my family. The kids that got to go home during summer breaks were from the more fortunate families who could afford to either pick up their children or pay for their transportation home. Otherwise, like me, kids spent summer breaks at the residential school, working and earning nothing. We had to clean the residence, paint the walls, scrub all the floors, work the gardens, mow the lawns.[30]

This is when I met one of the female supervisors.. She would give me treats, be nice to me, and then sneak me to her personal residence and play with me sexually. Don't forget, I had an idea by this time that this could happen because of what happened to me in Birtle. So, I used to have sex with her. Yet, I could never remember her name. But all in all, I thought that I had to do this or I would be in trouble if I did not obey her.

Then one day, around June of 1962, I got my first telephone call ever. It was a call from family back home. I was so excited at first. The principal came and got me out of the study hall and said I had an important phone call from my sister.[31] As it turned out, it was my worst telephone call ever. It was my cousin Phyllis Hewitt (née Cochrane) and my sister, Verna, calling to tell me that my mom had passed away on 12 June 1962.

I think I fell flat on the floor and fainted. The principal took the phone and spoke to Phyllis and Verna. My excitement quickly turned into a nightmare. I had never felt so alone and so helpless. All I thought about was that I would never see my mom alive again. I was so angry, and so upset, that I felt like killing myself.

I thought about the last time I saw her in the hospital when I was home for a summer break before moving to Portage la Prairie. Prior to my mom getting sick, she would blame me for stealing cigarettes despite never smoking a day in my life. While she was battling kidney disease, she tested me. She told me to take her last pack of cigarettes, but I cried and told her that I never smoked. She said, "Okay, I believe you now," and she was there waving from the window as I left the hospital. That was the last time that I saw my mother alive.[32]

Then came the time to attend my mother's funeral. I can't remember exactly, but I do remember the principal had two big men escort me back home. I had to be handcuffed to one of them at all times. I was not only embarrassed, but I felt like a prisoner. I could stay and visit my family, but I had to sit in between the two men through the funeral.

I was mad and hurt that I could not be with my friends and family. That was the only time that I ever returned home while I was at school. I could hardly recognize my family. I felt like a total stranger. They were looking at me in awe, like I had done something wrong at school. I was returned right away to "prison" – the residential school – the same day we buried my mother.[33]

Dauphin-Mackay Indian Residential School, 1945. P2012–08–199 Lindsay-Mackay Indian Residential School, Dauphin, Man., 1945. Used with permission, The General Synod Archives, Anglican Church of Canada.

The following year, I was transferred again, this time to Dauphin's Mackay Indian Residential School.[34] This was about 1963.[35] I was much older by then. I was a teenager. There, we had to walk to downtown Dauphin to attend daily classes. I forget the name of the school where I attended classes, but I remember we were treated fairly well, both at these schools and at the Mackay residence.

Abuses from staff members decreased but student bullying and hunger increased during my stay there. We were only given a small amount of poor-quality food such as macaroni and wieners. We had to supplement our diets by taking food from local gardens.[36]

When I came to Dauphin, I found things and people to be more kind and much more considerate. I was still mourning the loss of my mother. It was there and then that I realized that I would be alone forever. At that point, while I was walking alone down a street in Dauphin, Manitoba, I prayed to God and, in my prayer, I thought of my mother. I solemnly promised her that from that day forward, whatever I did, I would try to do my best. I promised to change my ways. To change my attitude. To walk the way she had dreamed of me to succeed. I cried like a baby the whole time I was making this promise.[37]

Up to this point, I was an average student, barely passing my grades. I had to cram in order to pass my exams. Things began to change for me. I started to fool around with the white girls. Many of them said they had a crush on me. I started dating a girl named Darlene, but I somehow felt inferior to her culture. I was "red" or darker than her. I remember walking down the streets trying to literally scratch the redness out of my arms. I don't know why I did this.

The following year, things really began to change for me. I got my very first recognition for being the "most improved student" from the previous year's performance. I was called up in front of all my classmates to receive my first certificate of achievement. After, when I was by myself, I cried to my mother's memories and said to her spirit, "You see, Mom, I told you I could do it. This is for you, and I will continue to be great for you. I wish you were here alive to be with me and see me accept this award. Thank you, Mom." The following year, I received certificates for the "highest marks" and the "best athlete of the year."[38]

From that time on, I seemed to excel in every competition I participated in. I used to run four miles every day, and I kept myself in shape. I started high school at Dauphin Collegiate and did the best I could in all my grades. I also played football for Dauphin Collegiate. I was a curling champion and I played hockey.

One of the most devastating memories from that time was when I was going with a girl. Her name was Penny. She was a white lady, and we were very close. I really cared about her. We could talk about some of my experiences in the schools and she got to know me very well. At that time, I was one of the most well-known athletes in town and passed as a white person due to my fair complexion, so her parents did not mind that we were going together.[39]

We were great for each other and she really loved me. One day, she wanted me to go with her and her friend for a car ride. Her friend's boyfriend had a really spruced-up car, like a Mustang, that his father had bought for him. She came to get me to go with her, but for some reason I felt that I had to study for my next day's exam. I told her to go ahead without me and that I would wait for her to come back.

She left, and that was the last that I ever saw her. Her friend's boyfriend was showing off his car and was speeding wherever they went. They went out of Dauphin on Hwy 10 towards Riding Mountain, and about two or three miles out, the guy was going so fast that he ran under a school bus that was letting some kids off. I guess this guy saw an oncoming vehicle and knew that he didn't have enough time to pass the parked school bus to be safe, so he decided to try to go on the right side of school bus, but he could not make it and ran underneath it, killing his girlfriend and mine. Believe it or not, the s.o.b. lived.

It was a horrific accident, brains and body parts spread all over the place at the accident scene. I had heard all the sirens from the town, and then Penny's parents came to see if their daughter was with me. I said, "No, she went for a ride with her friends," and they said, "Get in." We drove towards the accident scene. Police would not let anyone get too close to the scene. It was a horrible experience to see all of the blood, body parts, parts of the vehicle all over the place. To this day, I still have memories and nightmares about this, but I do not tell anyone. I manage to keep it to myself for my own reasons.

Now I was mourning the loss of two people, my mom and my girlfriend, but I had to carry on because of the promise I had made to my mother. I barely graduated high school, but for some reason I was happy with that, despite not making a high grade. I am sure my mother would have been very happy with my accomplishments, just the same.

4   AFTER GRADUATION

When I was released from school at the age of eighteen, it was like the system had released an animal or, in my case, a wolf, onto society.[1] I had graduated from high school and I was told that I was now on my own. I had to fend for myself. You have to understand that this was a completely foreign concept for me, having been institutionalized for sixteen of the first eighteen years of my life.

I was deprived of many of the skills that my family was supposed to teach me. I had to learn how to buy and wash my own clothes, to cook and find a place to live, all within a month of leaving the school.

Some of my fellow classmates and friends on the reserve were talking about moving to Thompson, Manitoba for work in the expanding nickel mines.[2] I was just worried about paying rent. I was never taught that you had to pay a monthly fee for a place to live.[3]

I had no bank account to make transfers from and thus no money to help pay rent. I was lucky that some of my older friends took care of me in this time period or I would have been homeless. I knew some other guys who were going to Thompson to work as well, Carl McCorrister, Colin Williams, and Wilfred Stevenson. We lived in an apartment until our paperwork for Thompson could be finalized, but we began realizing that we were never prepared for the outside world.[4] I also knew people from my home community of Peguis, including the late Kenny Sinclair, Alex Hudson, Dennis Stranger, and the late William McCorrister. One of my friends, the late Don LaForte, and my late former brother-in-law, Henry Lavallee, were also working there. This was enough incentive for me to want to go along.

I remember I had trouble passing the health test to work in the nickel mines. I was a few pounds too light, so I had to lie about my weight. I told the medical examiner that my weight fluctuated quite often. I could be five pounds heavier today and five pounds lighter next week. It was enough to convince him, and he passed me. I was the lightest man amongst us.

I was very excited about getting my first real job, and it paid big money. This was one of the highlights of my life. But at the same time, I was very nervous, especially when I realized that we were all separated on the job site and put to work in different areas with different shifts. The only time we would see each other was on weekends and paydays. I was told to never trust the banks as they could revoke your money at any time for being "Indian," so I was scared of opening an account and began hoarding all the money I earned.[5]

When I got my first paycheque, roughly $1,400 with numerous bonuses for working in the mine, I really didn't how to handle it. I had never had so much money in my life. I began to party with the boys, and I went wild, getting drunk, splurging, and throwing money at the waitresses in the bar. We would party in the basement suite where we were living. I did stupid things like throwing and smashing full bottles of beer against the walls, laughing, and saying things like "I never have to worry anymore, I have a good job now and I can afford to do this." When we would have a couple of days off together, the original group of classmates and friends from back home would get together and drink.

The first time I ever got drunk, the six of us bought twelve cases of beer and we drank them all in one night. Together we vented about the past and smashed countless bottles in anger over the things that had happened to us. After this night, I began drinking every chance I could, as the town of Thompson had nothing better for you to do on your time off.[6] So, like a fool, I would cash my cheques and just spend the money wherever I could. I did not realize why I did these stupid actions.[7]

Now, when I think about it, I can attribute my actions to my upbringing up in the residential schools. I was not prepared to handle success and independence. I would just blow my money foolishly. It seems that I was acting out at something, but could not figure it out.

I made so much money I didn't know what to do with it, I thought. I would hide my money in my mattress and all over in the place where I lived. It was not until I came to Winnipeg to visit my aunt, Nora Cochrane, who explained to me what banks were really for, that I understood it was the best thing to do with my money.

As it turned out, my first task at my new job was digging ditches underground at approximately 2,000 feet below surface. I really didn't like what I had to do, but this is the job a "green horn" or labourer gets when you had no previous mining experience. I would not say anything about how I felt or how nervous I was for fear of being laughed at by the other workers. As time went on, and as you gained experience, you earn the right to a better job and move up the seniority ladder.

It was not long before I worked my way up from the ditches to being a train master. I was hauling ore from the work areas to the chutes that brought the ore to the surface and to the mill. Then I was trained on how to transport dynamite and other explosives to the blasting areas, called stopes, where there were drillers waiting for their explosives.[8]

I talked my way into being a driller in a stope. I wanted to be there because there was more money to be made. The driller miners would make bonuses bigger than their regular hourly wages. I wanted to be one of them.

By this time, I had worked in the mine for about a year and a half, and things were looking up. I was working in the stopes, first as a mucker, the lowest position, then being on the drills. I was actually drilling eight- to ten-foot holes to be blasted. Then I became a stope leader, which is a prestigious position to be in when you're working in a mine. Fellow workers respected you and looked up to you as a leader and a good worker. This made me feel really proud of myself.

I worked as a stope leader for quite some time before I was moved up to an even higher position. Then I was asked if I would consider working in a little more risky and responsible job. That was reviving old stopes that were too dangerous to work in because of falling rocks and cave-ins, but still had lots of good ore that the company wanted to get at. Nickel mines were famous for "air blasts" or pockets of air and fumes that could be trapped in the rock after countless underground explosions and then potentially cause an unintended collapse.[9]

I was still not happy with life, however. I began to drink alcohol very heavily and became an alcoholic over time. I did not get along with too many people and got into a lot of fights at the local bar. If anyone looked at me the wrong way, he got a damned good licking. Now that I think about this, I am not very proud of it by any means. I really did not know how to handle life, because I didn't know what I wanted in life. It seemed like I was mad at the whole world and everyone in it. I did not realize that I was becoming a very volatile person.

Most stopes were left idle for about six months to a year before they would send a crew in to make them safe enough to work again. I was one of those men who set things up so that this workplace was safe enough for a regular crew to mine. I worked at this job for about a year. I was always nervous and on edge about my personal safety and had many close calls, near-death accidents that could have wiped my life out in a flash. We had to build massive wooden scaffoldings to help support areas that were weakened by the dynamite explosions or where cracks developed from the deadly air blasts, which could go off without any warning. We worked in small teams of two and my partner and I fixed three of these chutes in the mine to allow for more nickel mining.[10]

One day, I had had enough. On an assignment fixing a portion of the mine, I was almost caught in a major cave-in. We had managed to fix a significant crack in one of the shafts by constructing support beams onto the wall. Once fixed, our supervisors then called in the drillers to make twenty-four eight-foot holes to place sticks of dynamite in order to get the nickel ore out of the material we had salvaged. As my partner and I were the only ones who could certify that the area was secure, we would be the last ones to leave the shaft and ensure that all the sticks of dynamite had been successfully ignited. I began counting the sparks and immediately heard a louder rumbling than I was accustomed to, then I could see cracks forming around the walls we had supported to open the shaft in the first place. I was not sure whether to run down, or to run up as the cracks were forming on all sides of the walls, so I just grabbed the ladder and went up about sixty-five feet to the next level above the cave-in.

That close call took a chunk of my ankle and almost took my life. I was so shaken up I couldn't get my breath. I went up to the surface, threw my hard hat in my locker, had a shower, and told my supervisor, "This is my last time that I will ever go underground again in my life, and if I do go underground, it will be only six feet." My supervisor told me it was an accidental air blast, but I was too shaken up to go back down and wanted to work with my mind rather than my back. He asked me what I meant, and after hearing what had happened to me, he told me to take some time off, go see a doctor, and reconsider my position. But that was it. When I healed up, I left Thompson never to mine again. I was never compensated for the trauma and time off work while I healed up, as I had lasting impacts on my physical health, but also my mental health.[11]

I returned home to my Aunt Nora's in Winnipeg, Manitoba. When I got home, I had a few dollars. I went wild and drank steadily for a long,

long time. I am not even sure how long. It may have been at least a year and a half. I drank, fought, and partied, getting drunk in bars and at other people's homes. I was in bad shape and very depressed. I was a very angry person; I didn't know why I would fight and attack people. I was a confused person; I did not know what I wanted to do in life as I struggled with all my relationships. [12]

I ended up in jail many times for fighting and assaulting people in bars or on the streets. I was nothing but a troublemaker and a no-good, worthless person. So, at least, I thought. It got to the point that my aunt did not even want me at home if I was drinking.

Then one day in the early 1970s, while I was sobering up in jail, a judge did me a real great favour, although I did not think of it that way at the time. [13] The judge sentenced me to be on probation for some time and said that I would have to be assigned a sponsor, agree to go to Alcoholics Anonymous, and take recovery programming. At first, I resented this, but as time went on, I began to realize and see the good effects of recovery and how I was slowly accepting the change within myself. I began to think with a healthy, clear mind, and I began to feel healthy and good about myself once again.

I stayed with the program for quite a while and started releasing my anger out into boxing rather than on the streets. I realized that I had a significant problem with alcohol and in order to be a high-quality fighter, which I was thinking of becoming, I needed to lose weight and stop drinking. [14] Even when my time on probation was up and I was a free man again, I kept with the program and continued AA because I met very good people there who were genuine, helpful friends with good hearts.

I went back home to my Aunt Nora's in Winnipeg. She was very glad to see me and wanted me to continue with what I was doing. I always took her as my mom, most of my life since I was approximately eight or nine years old. She treated me like I was her very own son, maybe because she did not have a son.

At the time, I was broke and needed money, so I started to seek employment. I found work, which I really did not care about, and it wasn't long before my frustrations took over. I bounced from job to job and started to drink again. This time I thought that I could drink "responsibly and controllably." What a joke that was.

5 WORKING LIFE

I started my boxing career while I was staying with my aunt after leaving Thompson, Manitoba in the early 1970s. I trained and fought out of the old Royal Athletic Boxing Club in St Boniface, Winnipeg. I was eighteen when I first started and ended up boxing for about fifteen years. My boxing name was "Smokie" and I was the light middleweight Manitoba amateur boxing champion twice, Western Canadian Champion twice, and silver medallist in the Aboriginal Olympics.

During my boxing training, I got to travel quite a bit, but there was something still bothering me about my past. I was longing for – believe it or not – missing, even, the residential school system, and the regimented daily routine. I found out about the Armed Forces of Canada and I did some research on what they offered: security, a job to make money, a roof over my head, and three square meals a day. This sounded like something I thought would be ideal for me, and before I knew it, I had joined the Canadian Air Force Services, destined to be an aero technician, in 1968.

At first, I thought that the air force was the real "cat's meow." I was sent over to Cornwallis, Nova Scotia to take my basic training with hundreds of other potential servicemen. Basic training was a six-week period, and, boy, it was quite an ordeal. It was very hard. We could never answer with "Can't do it," "No," or "Later on." We were put on obstacle courses. For example, we had to run a five-mile obstacle course within one hour, and you stayed at that level until you made it. I remember one guy who was three seconds off and they refused to pass him. He was still at that level when the rest of us finished our basic training. I never did find out what happened to that fellow. This training course was to toughen us up and to make us appreciate the Canadian uniform we were wearing and be proud of it. I finally had an identity as an honourable military man, and I believed, for the first time in my life, that I was a part of something greater than myself.[1] For that training period, we could not watch TV, have any radios, or receive and read any mail. We could not have any books to read. All we could do was to work on our kits, our living quarters, and our uniforms.

After my basic training, I was posted to Camp Borden, Ontario. We were sent there to take our courses, in my case, those of an aero technician. I

Raymond, Air Force Portrait, 1967. Used with permission of Raymond Mason.

was told that the waiting list was too long. Instead, I had to take a course in cooking. Well, what a disappointment. To me, making me a cook was like trying put a square block into a round hole. Anyway, I went through the motions and passed the course and worked in the kitchen for a while, mostly peeling potatoes and making soup. I enjoyed the regimented style of life that resembled my experience in residential schools, as I knew that I would always have three meals a day and a bed to sleep in.

In my evenings and spare time, I kept on training for my boxing. At this time, I did not realize that the Armed Forces had done away with boxing altogether as a part of their services.[2] I learned later that they did away with boxing because there were too many boxers getting hurt, especially with head injuries. I just thought that the Forces weren't providing material for boxers to train, so I went along with a couple of guys who travelled to Toronto to train and fight at the Old City Boxing Club.

I did not realize how serious the Armed Forces took their position on boxing, but one night, the base commander saw me fighting on a card in Toronto. The next morning, I was called into his office. He said to me, "Great fight last night." "Oh yeah, did you come to see me fight?" I asked. I was feeling good about this because I had won my fight. "Sure did," he said, and then he let me have it. He said, "Don't you know the rules around here?" I said, "Yes, I think I do," and he said, "Like hell you do, you're being charged for insubordination."

While I was in Camp Borden, I was made lance corporal and was responsible for our platoon's living quarters. I had a problem with two members of my platoon. They were both pretty big guys who did not like me because I was Indian.[3] They would call me all sorts of nasty names, and did things to get me in trouble.[4] You see, when you are a lance corporal you are expected to be able to control your platoon at all times, no matter what. So, if my members did anything wrong, I would be in trouble for not handling the situation.

On one occasion, while I was away, they tipped over my entire dresser with all my personal belongings and began laughing when I was cleaning it up.[5] Then, one evening, I had enough of them. I usually assigned duties to help clean our quarters weekly and this one fell when both of these guys were together. When they were supposed to clean the floors, they made a mess instead by scratching the floors up and tipping my bed over and throwing my belongings all over my sleeping quarters.[6]

I went after the tallest one first, hit him in the jaw, knocking him through the big glass picture windows. He fell a story and a half, and it almost killed him. When he fell through the window, he also cut his head on some broken glass, just centimetres from a vein. As for the other guy, I caught him in our sleeping quarters and knocked him out cold. It wasn't long before the ambulance and the armed forces police arrived. I guess I must've really lost it because I blew my lid and did not remember all of the things I was doing once I went after them.[7]

I was charged with assault causing bodily harm, sentenced to sixty days in military prison at Valcartier, Quebec. That is one prison you don't want to ever serve time in. It is brutal to say the least. I did my time and got out on good behaviour in forty-five days.[8] This was extremely gruelling as we were made to march during every activity and every hour of the day. During my time in prison, I was responsible for cutting the grass and cleaning up garbage throughout the duration of my sentence, all the while marching to attention.[9]

When I got back to base, I was up in front of the base commander once again. Immediately I got scared. I thought, "Oh shit, what did I do now?" But that was when he told me that I was a very good boxer and that if I wanted to pursue it, I had to make a choice: quit boxing and stay in the Armed Forces, or continue boxing and resign from the Forces with an honourable discharge. I took the latter. Within twenty-four hours, I was on the train to Winnipeg, Manitoba. In essence, I only spent about two years in the armed forces but, let me tell you, I learned a lot about respecting that uniform and our servicemen, what they had to go through to wear that uniform and to serve our country.[1011]

When I was not training for boxing, I spent a fair bit of time drinking alcohol. Sadly, I was an alcoholic.[12] After I got out of the military, my sense of identity was lost and I could drink at any time not just on weekends or evenings.[13] I got into trouble, although nothing major. My Aunt Nora still did not want me home if I was drinking or drunk, so I just stayed away.

It seemed like I was a local celebrity because I was a good champion boxer. My friends kept giving me a place to stay, eat, and drink beer. I guess you could say this was a very sad time in my life. I really did not know what I wanted or where I was going. I was in and out of AA programs. Once I got healthy again and was back in shape, I would go back to drinking. When you were seen being drunk in public, you would be picked up, put in jail, and charged for being intoxicated in a public place. Boy, did I ever hit that place many times. Finally, after many, many times of being caught and charged by the same police officers and judge, they got to know me by name.

I struggled with this type of life for quite some time. Finally, I guess you could say that I realized I had hit my rock bottom. It seemed like I was finished, with nowhere to turn, nowhere to go, nobody to help.[14] I just wanted to end my life, and I tried to commit suicide one or two times.

The time I got the closest was during this period and it's still difficult to write or talk about. I remember that I was depressed and believed I had not lived up to the promise I had made to my mother and myself. For a period of about three weeks that year, I stayed in a small studio apartment eating only peanut butter, lettuce, and water. I later found out that I was undergoing a nervous breakdown coupled with severe depression as I lost track of the days and everything seemed to be piling up. I thought that I would never obtain a job again due to my drinking and began having terrible nightmares on the rare occasion that I could sleep. I dreamed about ending my life so that I could go track down and hurt some of the abusers from my time in school. On one occasion, I put a shell into a gun and put it under my chin, but the gun misfired. Thank God I never succeeded. I guess He had other plans for me, which I still had not figured out.[15]

Again, I went back to my Aunt Nora's. She and my Uncle Lawrence were still living in Winnipeg. I sobered up and went straight for quite a while. I started to take the boxing more seriously. I trained and ate the right food every day, my auntie made sure of that. I would jog every day, and she was my timekeeper. We sure had lots of fun. She found it so funny when I was stretching and limbering up before going on my five-mile run. I used to be in tremendous shape.

Sometimes, my aunt would forget about keeping time, so she would make it up and say that I had run the course in so many minutes. She would say, "You ran real fast today my boy." She did not tell me that she very seldom marked the exact time for me until much later. We had so much fun laughing. She was laughing at me because of what she did, and I was laughing at her for how hard she was laughing and how funny she looked. Anyway, I let her get away with it.

I really loved my Aunt Nora, because she loved me and treated me as if I was her own son. She would always worry about me, about my safety. She always wanted me to stop drinking, and always wanted me to come home. That way, she knew I was safe, and she wouldn't have to worry. Her passing on was a big loss. It left a very big void in my heart. I miss her so much.

Shortly after her passing, I met Sharon and we got married.[16] At first, I thought that I was in love. We had two sons and adopted our daughter during the time I was working for Swan Lake First Nation. At that time, we were living in a rented farm home in between Treherne, Manitoba, and Swan Lake First Nation.

During our marriage, we had a lot of problems. After a couple of years or so, things weren't going well. I realized that we were very incompatible even though I tried to change my ways of living. First it was my drinking. I quit that. Then I took an interest in hunting and fishing, but that took me away from home too often. I wanted independence with friends and other relationships, but marriage needs compromise. Overall, my marriage was not a healthy situation.

We endured our marriage for a number of years. We had a lot of breakups over the years, I've lost count of how many. Anyway, I would end up getting lonesome for my home and my children, so I would continue to try to compromise in order to continue as family. Things would go well only for a short while.

In the meanwhile, I continued looking for normal work. Some of those jobs that I worked during this period included ABC Construction – labourer; Manitoba Sugar – labourer; and Domtar Construction – labourer/forklift operator.

The money was nowhere as good as the mining job that I first held in Thompson, but it was enough to go back to drinking again. I knew it was wrong for me. I kept thinking about the AA program and the wonderful people that I'd met there. I kept my distance from them because I knew that they would be disappointed in me because I started to drink alcohol once again, even though at the same time I knew they would support me.

This type of living kept up for a year or so, then I decided to go back to school. I kept thinking of the promise that I had made to my mom. I started to check out the different places where I could study. I decided to take a business administration course at Success College on Portage Avenue in Winnipeg because they were offering training courses in business administration. I thought I would need this if I wanted to be a successful businessman. It was a two-year course, but you could finish it sooner, at your own speed, depending how fast and how hard you worked. It took only one year for me to finish this course, and I graduated with a diploma.

I went to work for some time after that, as before, but I wanted something better. I started to think about taking a course in business at university somewhere. I did some research and found out that if I took commerce at the university level, it was the highest level of business administration a person could achieve.

I got accepted as a mature student at the University of Manitoba.[17] By this time, I was already getting up in age. I think I was around forty years old in the 1980s. I passed my first year arts course and then majored in commerce. There were very few Indigenous students going to the University of Manitoba at that time, and I often felt alone and a little inferior to the other students. I told myself that I had to prove to my fellow students that I was just as smart as they were. I worked hard to achieve high marks to show them that an Indigenous student could be just as smart as they were. It was a tough course, but I managed to finish with a degree in five years.

During some of the semesters that I was at University of Manitoba, I would work part-time at the Department of Indian and Northern Affairs in the Economic Development Department. I had a great time learning how the government worked to serve our people. Bureaucratic ways and attitudes to work were evident to me while working here. During other semesters, I would go over to work for the provincial government in the Department of Northern Affairs, servicing the Métis people of Manitoba in the area of economic development. I remember a regional director of Northern Affairs telling us, "Don't forget, we have the almighty dollar, so we do what we want to do; they don't get to tell us how we do our jobs." This attitude towards Indigenous people made our job harder.

As part of this job, I made trips to reserves. On one of our first trips up north to a reserve in Manitoba, we flew with a float plane into a remote community for orientation alongside a department head. Since these planes were rare, some people converged on the dock to greet the VIP from the Department of Indian and Northern Affairs. He told the people that he wanted to see the chief, so they took him to a beach where most of the community was lying down in a form of protest.

The chief was there. He told the department head to leave the community immediately but spoke to me and said, "Take the bullshit back with you." I quickly tried to take control of the situation and helped escort him back to his plane before something occurred.[18]

When I finished my education, I was damn glad I didn't have to work for government for the rest of my career. Because of this it confirmed the attitudes of the "white bureaucrats" towards the Native people. It doesn't matter if you're Metis, Inuit, Treaty Status Indian, or a Non-Treaty Status Indian. These positions all helped me learn how to work with people, manage accounts, and organize travel to all parts of the country. These skills would become invaluable as I started to begin my search for reconciliation.

While I was still working at Swan Lake First Nation, Sharon and I started to talk about developing our own business and becoming our own bosses.

We weren't sure what type of business we wanted to start, so I started to do the research on what would be the best avenue to take. It was about the same time I patented my moose invention, an idea that I got from my late grandfather, Albert Edward Prince. It was a very simple but very effective way of luring in the moose. It was a soup can with a hole punched in the middle of the bottom and had a string (skate lace) through it with a knot tied so that it could not slide through the hole. You wet the string and pull it through your hand to create a vibration and the sound of a moose calling.

Shortly after patenting the moose call at around 1984, we set up a sporting goods business. We also sold other sporting goods to complement our main mover, the moose call, including tanning items, sport t-shirts, tanning lawn chairs, etc.[19] We sold thousands of moose calls right across Canada. We sold distribution rights across Canada to sporting and hunting businesses on consignment.

Our moose call was introduced to the world when we rented a booth at the World Trade Show in Montreal. The World Trade Show is an event where all businesses meet from around the world, get together to showcase their products and items. To attend this kind of event you must be a member of the World Trade Show Association.

Sharon and I were still having our marital problems. We broke up again about that time, and I moved alone to an apartment in Winnipeg. This was also when I got in trouble with the sales component of our business. You see, when we sold our moose calls on consignment, we were expected to pay all the sales taxes up front, which I could not do. However, I was paying the sales tax as I was receiving the payments for sales.

This was not good enough for the government; they had their rules and they wanted their money right away. I fought them in courts for as long as I could. The courts would not understand that I sold my moose calls on consignment and was paying the sales tax as I got paid for the sales that took place.

Finally, one day, I got a visit from three big gentlemen, Revenue Canada agents. They stormed into my office, took all my receivables, payables, and any paper that had any kind of writing on it. When they were done, they left me with nothing but blank pieces of paper and my phones. They sent my employees home that day. It's a day I will never forget. I suppose this is what you would call a "foreclosure on my business." They took all the information they wanted and left me with nothing to operate my business.

I was, in a way, forced to close the business until Revenue Canada got what they wanted, regardless of what we said or had done.

They left with boxes and boxes of my business documents. What they did after that destroyed my business because they wrote a "demand note," calling a third-party collection agency to demand to all my consignment customers to either pay the sales tax to them or return all unsold moose calls to us. This was quite a terrible experience, and I was forced to shut down my business. I later sold my moose call patents to a German company that I knew of through one of my former salesmen. They had an office somewhere in Winnipeg, Manitoba for a while. I really don't know what they did with the moose call.

Approximately three weeks to a month later, I received all my documents back from Revenue Canada. They called me to go pick them up. I realized that the money that was left in a bank account after they lifted their hold, or freeze, was quite substantial, but my business was virtually dead. I used some of the profits from our moose call to qualify for funding from Indian Affairs to purchase a strip mall at Libau, Manitoba. This business had towing, propane and gas sales, a service garage, restaurant, grocery supplies, and liquor outlet.

I successfully applied for a business grant from Indian and Northern Affairs' Economic Development Department. We named it Mason's Trading Post, and I did a lot of major renovations. We put in a new paved parking lot, new flooring, new dividers, new show cases, a new kitchen, new stove and fridges, new walls in certain areas, and also a new sewer system with a new septic field and new bathroom facilities. In the garage, we put in two new vehicle bays new tire changing machine, and other new equipment that was necessary. When we took over the business, the former owner was doing something like $175,000 in gross sales. Our gross sales in the first year were approximately $1.3 million. We thought that in order to make money, we had to spend money and work very hard.

We had a thriving business, but that's when my domestic situation soured. When life showed promise one way, other challenges arose. Sharon and I had difficulties with family and the way that they took advantage of us as business owners. We decided to sell the Trading Post for a good sum that included stock and inventory, which we used to buy a house at West St Paul, Winnipeg. We paid cash for our home, and it was beautiful.

We decided that if we went to church, it would help our relationship. Sharon felt that going to church would help me with my alcohol problems.

Things did not turn out as well as we had hoped. I was beginning to get bored with life and, through church, I met John, who would feed my interest in new business opportunities at the time.

John knew I had money. He came to me and asked if I would help him and lend him $10,000 for six months so that he could start a new year of roofing business. I wanted to see his operation first because I didn't know anything about a roofing business. As it turned out, his equipment was as old as the hills, but I couldn't have known at the time. John invited me into his house. It was a very poor home. His children didn't have food to eat or, at least, very little. Well, being a Christian man, I felt really sorry for those kids, and was thinking about them more than the business. My heart melted, and I felt that I had to do something to help them.

I didn't realize that John was not being entirely honest and that he was also an alcoholic. He sure had me fooled. I believed in him because I always saw him in church every Sunday, singing and praising the Lord, repenting for his sins. I didn't realize that during the week he was drinking and playing guitar and singing in the local bars. This was definitely a no-no in our church.

After I loaned him the money for his business, he was back within four months asking for another loan from me, when he had not even made one payment on the first loan I gave him. I said to him, "Wait a minute, before I give you another dime, I want to look at your records and your operation." As it turned out, he never had any records to speak of; all he had were boxes of receipt books as a record of receivables and jobs he was successful in getting. It was a very poor recording system.

I quickly realized that to protect and to get back the money I had given him, I had to be a 50/50 partner in his business. It took a little while, but he decided that he would take me on as a partner. So, I had to learn about the roofing business very quickly. As everything turned out, I had to break up the partnership because he took too much money from our company and me. Up until this time John did not invest any money on his part and the equipment, as I found out, was worthless. I would prefer not to get into the details of this mess.

This was about in the late 1980s, when I decided that I must go on my own, so Mason's Roofing, Construction & Renovation Services came to fruition. I took a couple of the more knowledgable and veteran roofers with me to help me learn more about the business. I purchased all new roofing equipment, to the tune of about $650,000 to $700,000. All my workers really liked working for me because they took pride in working with new equipment and I paid them fair wages. I was always considerate of my workers. I treated them with respect. Word got out how good it was working for me, so that many roofers wanted to work for me. A short time later, I added on renovation services because of the demand.

I later tendered a bid for roofing repairs in Edmonton, Alberta, for an insurance company that was co-ordinated from Calgary, Alberta called Travellers Insurance. Apparently, their head office was in Toronto, Ontario. Still, all the invoices and P.O.s were sent from the Calgary office.

The contract was worth approximately $750,000 dollars, according to my calculations. Plus, I picked up jobs from people who were not Travellers Insurance customers. That work was worth approximately another $500,000. There was a high demand for roofing at that time because Edmonton had been hit by a tornado and had a lot of damage. My firm was successful in obtaining a contract to do roofing repairs for Travellers. I had to move a portion of my business to Edmonton, leaving enough equipment and personnel to work with my wife Sharon so that they could complete work and continue business in Winnipeg and the rest of Manitoba.

Things were going along very well. For a while at least. My marriage was falling apart again, largely because of a lack of trust. At the same time, I was so damn busy I hardly had time to sleep. I was responsible for about 250 shingle and cedar roofers/clean-up men/roof-strippers, seventy-five flat and hot-tar roofers, and fifty corrugated metal roofers.

I tried to keep all my men together, so I rented the whole East Glenn Motor Hotel and another hotel – I can't remember the name – just down the street from where we were. It was quite a task to keep my men together because they liked to drink and party a lot. Payday was every Friday, so I set up an office in my room for office personnel to look after the invoicing, payroll, and disbursements for me.

Everyone was happy except for me. I was burnt out, plus my domestic life was not a happy one. I headed back to Winnipeg, leaving the Edmonton operation to one of my best and most trusted employees. When I got home, my clothes were packed and left outside the front door.

By this time, everyone had had enough of our marital problems. They were affecting work. We lost the contract for all the Travellers Insurance roofing repair jobs in Edmonton, Alberta. We were left with completing the private roofing jobs that we'd luckily picked up while repairing roofs for that contract. These people were not Travellers Insurance customers but still needed to have their roofs repaired. They hired my firm to repair their roofs as well; this amounted to approximately 500 plus jobs.

I also got word that the Canadian Pacific Railway also cut our contract in Winnipeg, Manitoba. That meant a loss of $750,000.00 in business. Well, that was it. Work and home life were too difficult. I was determined to call it quits on our marriage for good.

I started to drink again, and boy, did I hit the bottle hard. I moved back home to my Aunt Nora's. My children would phone me in Winnipeg and cry, asking me to come back home because they were lonesome for me. It was very hard on me and on everyone. I knew if I went back to that situation, things would not change. I knew that I had to take care of myself for the time being.

One beautiful morning I left Winnipeg for Edmonton, Alberta, not knowing when I would get there or where I was going to end up. I took my time. I stopped in Saskatoon, Saskatchewan, and went out drunk for a week before I sobered up to continue on to Edmonton. As it turned out, things got even worse for me.

This was the beginning of the real "dark ages" of my life. Before this trip, I did not dream that I would ever be living in the Edmonton area for six or seven years at this point in my experiences. I would travel back and forth to Winnipeg whenever I could, mostly to work on the dream of seeking recognition, justice, and compensation for the abuses we suffered at Indian residential schools through my work at Spirit Wind. And, so, I still managed to keep in touch with my fellow schoolmates, the ones who were working with me on Indian residential school issues.

I would stay in touch with one or two of them by phone or on some occasions I was able to make a few meetings in person. Soon after, I started another roofing business in Edmonton with one of the friends I had met, the chief of Ermineskin, one of the First Nations of Hobbema, Alberta. We became business partners. We did a lot of business around Edmonton and the surrounding area.

Then, I met and fell in love with a young lady who would change my life again. She lived in Edmonton but came from Lac La Biche, Alberta. Her name was Lisa.[20] Lisa had two daughters and one young boy with her. I did not know about her kids when we first dated, but we got along really well and eventually moved in with each other. I accepted her children and took them as if they were my own.

We got along well, but also had to deal with some bad habits, including going to bingo and the casino almost every day. I had to take financial advances from our business, and this, as I soon realized, got of hand. My business partner gave me an ultimatum because, by this time, I was also gambling and drinking way too much again.

It seemed I could not quit what I was doing. I got in trouble with the law a few times. So, we shut down our roofing business, and we had nothing to supply our habits. We ended up on welfare. That was not a very good experience for me. I hated it and was really embarrassed at myself for not being able to provide for my family.[21] Lisa and I started to argue a lot then, because we could not continue the lifestyle we'd had before. She would take off and leave me for days, and I would continue to drink around. Life was very difficult. I was charged for impaired driving on two different occasions, and I was waiting for trial on them when I got caught driving drunk again, a third time.[22]

I knew that if I didn't smarten up, I would be going to prison for a long time (three to six years). In order to start my rehabilitation, I had to first break up and leave my relationship with my common-law wife and go to AA meetings.

I met an AA member who was from back home, the late Mr Bill Cochrane, who really understood me and knew what I was going through. He helped me a lot. He got me a place to live at another AA member's place. This person was from Pine Falls, Manitoba.

I never felt so good in my life. For the first time in a long time, I was sobering up and thinking straight once again. By this time, I had been back in AA for almost a year.

I knew that I had to settle my three impaired charges, so I went to my lawyer and asked him if I could deal with all three charges together as one, and if he could put them off for another year. He was successful in doing that. This was when I decided to better and upgrade my computer and accounting capabilities so that I could get a fairly good office job again. By this time, I was unsure as to whether I could still do what was expected in an administrative office job. Do not forget, "If you don't use it, you lose it."

I was successful in getting accepted to take a computerized accounting course at the local CDI College, within walking distance from where I lived. I knew that if I did well in this course and proved that not only to myself, but also to others like my AA sponsor, Bill Cochrane, and my lawyer, it would also help me with my court trial. If I did well, maybe the judge would give me a break and let me stay out of prison.

As it turned out, I got the second highest marks in all of the college. These were also the highest ever for an Aboriginal student. I was doing very well and felt very proud of myself. When it came time for the trial on my DUI charges, I still had about two or three months of school before I had completely finished it. I asked my AA sponsor and my CDI director if they would come to support me in court, and vouch for me as to how good I was doing, that I was definitely working on bettering my life.

The judge was understandably not very kind with me. He gave me supreme hell and told me that if I wasn't going to AA meetings and college to clean up my act, he would have locked me up and thrown away the keys. He said, "Mr Mason, can you give me one good reason why I shouldn't send you in that door and throw away the keys?"[23] I said, "I realized that I have a problem with alcohol and need to improve, I am going to AA and church now and see a big difference. In addition, I have enrolled in a computer accounting class in college without missing a day and I am achieving the highest marks of any Aboriginal. I know I have done wrong and I am prepared to face the consequences."[24] After my AA counsellor said a few words, the judge made his decision. He said, "For the first time in all my life being a judge, I'm doing something I've never done before, and that is to let someone like you walk."[25] He gave me a three-year probation, compelled me to go see a psychiatrist, and gave me a fine for $4,000 to pay over three years. I had to continue AA meetings, make monthly reports to a Court Probation Officer, and complete my course at CDI College.[26]

Let me tell you, I was so nervous and shaking in my boots, I could hardly talk. I thanked him so much and promised that I would abide by the sentence and would not let him down. If I did, I would be letting my friends and myself down as well. I thanked him for his consideration and giving me another chance to make a change in my life.

Soon after that, I completed my course and got an office job working at Poundmaker's Lodge, an addiction treatment centre in St Albert, Alberta, on the outskirts of Edmonton. While I was working at my new job, I was very happy and very proud of myself. I was given time to go see my psychiatrist, Ms Grace Cook, also of St Albert. I spent the next two-and-a-half years seeing her. This was another high point in my life, because I spent time talking just about myself and my whole life history. I give her all the credit in helping me find the true "Raymond Mason."[27] I talked about my life in residential schools and the abuses I lived through up until that time. I felt that I was cheated in life, because I could never figure out why I had lost all these golden opportunities to make it in life, and to be better off financially, mentally, and emotionally.

I continued to work at my job and spend time seeing my psychiatrist. I couldn't figure out why she just wanted me to sit there and talk about my life. Then one day it was as if someone flicked a light switch on. I began to cry. I said to myself, "Oh, so that is the reason why I am the way I am, this is the reason why I treated my children and my first wife the way I did. I had severe mental illnesses from my time in the residential school and it helped explain the reason I blew all those golden opportunities."[28]

I finally realized why I was the kind of father I was rather than the father I should have been. I realized that because of the way I was brought up in a residential school as only a number, I was never nurtured, loved, or taught by a parent. It was impossible for me to know how to be a parent to my own children. I finally realized I was one of the worst fathers ever.

I did not know how to handle success. It was a new revelation in my life: I had "found myself," the real Raymond Mason. Now I understood what the residential school system and abuses did to me. I did not realize that the legacy of abuse, neglect, and loneliness had changed me on some level. I remembered when I didn't want to be Indian while I was dating the white girls, because, sadly, at that time, I was ashamed of being Native. Now I knew why I was so confused, angry, and bitter with life.

This revelation made me a new and different person. It was just like turning to a new page when you're reading a book. All the answers to my problems came in front of me in the blink of an eye. I cried and cried for hours. I knew I had to get busy and go back and make amends and apologize to many people, including my children, for the hurtful things I did and said to them.[29]

When I finished my computer accounting course, I did not hang around Alberta too much longer. I needed to get back to my homeland and start the long work of making amends to a few important people. Many of them accepted my apology, many didn't, and a few had passed on by this time. For the ones who did not accept my apology, I felt that I had done my part in trying to make things right, so I left it at that.

Shortly after I arrived back to Winnipeg, I stayed and lived with my sister, Verna Sinclair. It was not long before I got hired on with Swan Lake First Nation. My friend and boss, the late Mr Roy McKinney, put me on part-time work on project and community development.

Once again, I was a happy, sober, and proud working man. I did a lot of travelling back and forth from Winnipeg to Swan Lake for about a year and a half. I used to go visit my Aunt Nora and Uncle Lawrence a lot. Remember they're the ones who adopted me and loved me as if I was their very own. Shortly after that, Uncle Lawrence took sick and they moved him to the Peguis Personal Care Home for a couple of years. Sadly, it was there he passed away. What a big loss this was to our family.

When we were making funeral arrangements for my uncle at the Peguis Band Office, I met my beautiful and wonderful wife, Rhoda Mae Forster. To this day, I can't figure out what she was doing there, but it sure was a good thing for me. I began to talk to her, not realizing that she had lost her husband about two years earlier. I asked her if she came to Winnipeg once in a while. She said "yes." We had previously known each other in the first grade in Peguis Day School but she was never sent to the residential school.[30] I often wonder how much different my life would be if I stayed in that day school with Rhoda. She taught me how to be a better parent and keeps track of nearly thirty grandchildren's birthdays. I never celebrated my birthday until I was twenty-six, so I never learned how to celebrate family things and I thank her every day for the love and knowledge she has provided.[31]

That is when I asked her if we could get together and have coffee. She said, "sure," so we exchanged telephone numbers and planned to meet in Winnipeg sometime later in the following weeks. Before I met Rhoda, I always prayed to meet someone from back home, someone who would love me just the way I am. When I met her, to me it was like a dream come true. We talked openly about my reputation as a "drunk" and how my experiences in the residential schools had influenced the terrible decisions I had made in my life.[32]

We dated and courted each other for about two years, and then one day, I decided that I would have a surprise engagement party at my niece's place on Logan Avenue in Winnipeg. So I invited some friends over and told them what I was up to. I told them and my niece that I was going to surprise Rhoda, get down on one knee and ask her if she would marry me. The excitement got started, plans really kicked into gear. One of my friends looked after the booze situation and the girls looked after the cooking. Meanwhile, Rhoda thought that we were going to have one big party, not realizing it was for her and me. That's when I asked her if she would marry me. She said, "Yes!" Boy, I was elated.

At first, my wife's children, the girls, did not really accept me or take to me right away. I could not expect anything different. They had lost their father just two and a half years before. When Rhonda and I started dating, I knew and expected to get some friction from them. I respected that the loss was still hard for them. I let them say whatever they wanted to say to me. I knew that this would be a battle for a while, because I had to prove myself to them (the girls), to show them that I would take care of and love their mother. It took some time for this to take place. Today, things are so nice and different with the girls. Now, if their mother gets mad and tries to argue with me, who's here to stick up for me? It's the girls.[33]

As for my wife's son, Keith, well, it's a different story. He never says anything mean, even to hurt a fly. We got along right from the start. We used to have a few drinks of beer together, laugh, and joke around with each other. In fact, when Rhoda and I were first going out, we used to spend time together at his house. The girls would ask if we were at his place, but he would hide us and deny that we were there together over the weekends. I will always love Keith, the girls, and their families. I take them as if they were my very own. I am very proud to have them as my family. I made a personal promise that I will not miss what I missed with my own children and grandchildren while they were growing up. I will not miss all the good things you see in a child as they grow up.

My marriage with Rhoda has taught me a lot of wonderful things, especially how important family is in your life – playing cards, visiting, birthday parties, and other special occasions that I had missed out on. I never celebrated my birthday until I was a grown adult because I always thought that your birthday is just another day in your life. None of the family members ever thought about it either, I guess. Either I was not home or was not around. My birthday, and other holidays like Christmas, New Year's, Easter, was just another day for me. I guess you would say that, when you're in a residential school, things like that did not matter much at all.

Soon, I decided to move back to Peguis First Nation, my permanent home.[34] I had never been so happy. Rhoda and I started a local business, R.M. Forster Enterprises, where we carried on business with dry cleaning services, linen and doormat rentals, and janitorial equipment and supplies and services.

We tried to offset the loss of business in our local community by expanding to other First Nation communities farther north. Business picked up again, but the distance meant high travel costs that proved to be more than we expected. The business began to suffer as time went on. Because we could not afford higher wages, it was hard to maintain good staff, and it was getting harder for us to work ourselves. We were getting older, and it was hard to carry on the business, so we decided to close the doors in September of 2009. We tried to sell our business, but no one could afford to buy it from us, so we just sold whatever we could, the vehicles, the equipment, and the products at garage sale prices.

While we operated our business, I was able to work and travel to all areas of Canada, to promote and expose Survivors' calls for justice, and meet and negotiate with the dignitaries and politicians who brought about the Indian Residential School Settlement Agreement. There was a lot of behind-the-scenes activity that had to happen to get that agreement done. Now I was able to be free and work more diligently on the Spirit Wind dream.

At the same time, I carried on a small business in private consulting, business proposal development, business advising, bookkeeping and accounting, community development, and source funding for all projects within the community. At the present time I work with Chief Glenn Hudson and council to better our community and have economic stability.

6   SPIRIT WIND

When I arrived back in Winnipeg in the late 1980s, the first thing I did was find the boys – the original five, my first committee – to restart our journey towards justice, compensation, and an apology from Canada. I could not find all of them. As I later found out – sadly – two of them had passed away, and we had just lost touch with Clifford Kematch. So, I had to form another committee that was willing to get together for the same cause. For the new committee, I wanted one that would represent the whole province, so I invited the following, and they accepted:

Charles Harper to represent the northeastern part of Manitoba
David Chaske to represent another part of northern Manitoba
Ms Marina Tacan to represent Sioux Valley First Nation and area –
    still with us today
Ms Ruth Roulette from Long Plain First Nation to represent the
    Dakota Ojibway Tribal Council and area – still with us today
Melvin Swan for the southern part of Manitoba – still with us
    today on an ex officio basis because of his current medical state
I, Ray Mason, to represent Peguis First Nation and southern
    Manitoba

We held our meetings at the St Regis Hotel restaurant or wherever we could find space to sit and talk about our issues. We began by naming our organization as the Manitoba Indian Residential School Movement. We talked to many former residential school students who supported us 100 percent. That's when we decided that we would need the help of our Native leadership and also the help of a lawyer.

We decided that we would go talk to our chiefs and our leadership to see if they would support us with some in-kind donations by lending us an office and phone to use. Instead, we got the "cold shoulder." When I went and spoke to the Assembly of Manitoba Chiefs, I remember them actually laughing at my presentation. Then I walked out of the room very disgusted and upset. I felt very disrespected by that chief.

I walked the streets of Winnipeg in search of a lawyer. This took a very long time, something like three to five years to get someone who would help us and take on our case. Some of the lawyers we talked to wanted a $100,000 deposit, some $80,000, and so forth, before they would consider doing anything. Well, of course, we never had a hope in hell to come up with that kind of money.

Finally, after so many attempts and years past, in 1994 we got a lawyer who would listen to us and actually believed we had a case. I am not sure how we found Mr Dennis Troniak of Troniak Law Office, but it was the best thing that could have ever happened to us. It was like a Godsend because, by this time, we were beginning to get really discouraged about everything and wondering if we would ever secure a lawyer who would help us.[1]

Before Dennis Troniak took our case, I remember going and sitting with him for approximately two and a half hours in his office, explaining the different events of abuses that I went through, also all my experiences I had when I attended Birtle, Portage la Prairie, and Dauphin McKay Indian residential schools. He was writing everything down while I was talking, and after I was done, he said, "Leave it with me. I think you may have something here. I will look into it and let you know." I never felt quite so elated and so happy. I thought to myself, "Thank God. We now have a lawyer." I left his office with goose bumps all over my body and, when I got outside on the street, as I walked home, I began to cry with joy. Because, I never thought that this would ever come to pass. We had so many highs and lows along the way thinking, each time, that "for sure, we have a lawyer" when we didn't. Up until then, lawyers seemed to lead us on, making us think that they would work for us, and end up not taking our issues seriously enough to take on the task.

A short while later, I told my committee members that we had a lawyer who was willing to look into our case. We all started to laugh with joy, and Mel led us in a prayer to thank our Creator for finally giving us a lawyer who was willing to help us. I told the committee that I personally felt that this would be our man. There was something about him that made me feel confident, even though we didn't have any money. He was so compassionate and considerate of our situation and issues. He also gave us office space to use for our meetings, sometimes paying for boardroom space in the same building where he had his law firm if he was using his own.

I kept on working, and I travelled across the country to spread the word that Canada had done us wrong by trying to assimilate us and putting us in these institutions they called schools. I travelled to northern Manitoba, then to Ontario, Saskatchewan, Alberta, and British Columbia. I was gathering a lot of support wherever I went. Many agreed with the goals of our committee and wanted to get involved in some way.

The travel was to try and gain exposure and support from other Survivors who had experienced the same types of abuses. We wanted to represent people who may not have had the opportunity to have lawyers hear their case, and in order to stand together to face Canada we needed to have a large number of other Survivors. We believed this was the only way to achieve a national voice so that Canada would be forced to listen to our complaints.[2]

These trips were emotional, but also filled my spirit with hope and determination that we could help these people seek justice on our own terms. I remember when we went to Pine Creek, Manitoba to meet with Survivors from the Pine Creek Residential School as particularly difficult. A former professional hockey player, who was known as being a big tough guy, attended the gathering and cried like a baby. He told us that he dreamed of having the chance to have revenge against his abusers and wished he could hurt them all.[3] These events were always painful as I talked about my own personal abuse and heard hundreds of other stories that were similar or worse than mine. During a visit to Winnipeg, I had heard that one of my former abusers had come to the event in hopes of disputing some of the accusations that students were making against him. I saw him for a second but he disappeared into the crowd and it took everything in my power not to chase him and try to hurt him for what he had done not only to me but countless other grassroots people.[4] However, these experiences drove me to seek justice that could help these brave people in a manner that did not put Survivors in jail.

Part of the drive and desire to keep working came from the fact that the government of Canada had, at that time, apologized to and was compensating Japanese-Canadians for their internment during the Second World War. We thought Canada should damn well pay for what they did to us (Treaty Indian people of Canada) and to compensate us for all the abuses we suffered in their colonial institutions that they called schools, "while trying to take the Indian out of the child." This was enough incentive to keep me angry enough to keep my drive alive to the very bitter end. I am determined even to this day that I would never quit, not until we (both residential school and day school Survivors) receive justice, financial compensation, and an apology. A commitment to educate the rest of the country and the world as to what happened to the Indigenous people of Canada because of Indian Residential Schools was also requested and maintained throughout the process.

Somewhere around this time, I came across an article that contained a quote by a government official, Duncan Campbell Scott, who was the deputy superintendent general of the Department of Indian Affairs of Canada. From the 1920 excerpt of his testimony it stated, "I want to get rid of the Indian problem. I do not think as a matter of fact, that the country ought to continuously protect a class of people who are able to stand alone … Our objective is to continue until there is not a single Indian in Canada that has not been absorbed into the public body and there is no Indian question, and that there is no Indian Department, that is the whole object of this Bill."[5]

I got cold shivers throughout my entire body as I finally realized what those Indian agents were trying to do when they took me from my family. The final puzzle piece clicked and it was apparent that the reason I experienced so many horrible abuses was simply to get rid of our culture, language, and people so that Europeans culture, language, and people could replace us. I also knew what I had to do then, and why I would never stop my fight in protection of the culture, language, and grassroots people.[6] Canada almost succeeded, and this alone was enough to keep our drive and our spirit alive to see that Canada must "make good" and to clear up their history about what they did to us in those days, one of the greatest "black eyes" in the history of Canada.[7]

Many people have asked what it was that made me stay with this cause for all these years when others would have given up. I must say that I have had many, many setbacks, including the deaths of some of my original committee members, God bless their souls. I am sure that what I am doing today, they would have agreed 100 percent with me. Because we had no money or pertinent resources, it made it that much harder for the committee members to work together. They have dedicated so much of their personal time because they believe that Canada has an obligation to make all things right to all Survivors.

Shortly after we engaged Mr Dennis Troniak as our legal counsel, he called to tell me that we could not sue our government. We were told that you cannot sue your own government. At first, this was a devastating blow like you would never believe. I thought that the world had come to an end. It knocked me into numbness and I couldn't even think straight for quite some time. This was such a setback that I thought that I would not be able to handle it and pick up the pieces in order to move forward with this cause.

I thought about this for some time, and then our spiritual adviser, Melvin Swan, told me to go see an Elder and seek advice from him. He would have an answer for us. I agreed, and sought out Elder Dave Murdock from the Fisher River Cree Nation. I went and spent time with him and prayed with him, and then he told me to leave it with him for seven days. He said he needed to go into the bush for seven days to fast and pray on it: "I will have an answer for you at that time."

At this time, after some recent research, I was under the impression that it was our group that gave Canada the "big shove" to make them admit that they had done us wrong by putting us in these colonial institutes called the IRS schools and different church schools. I say this because, after spending time with the Elder, he reaffirmed that what Canada tried to do to us was to "take the Indian out of the Child," in other words, "cultural genocide."[8]

With this new revelation, I thought that if Canada does not come to the bargaining table and deal with us to do the right thing, then I would go to the World Courts in The Hague and charge Canada with cultural genocide, not to mention "Child Abduction" as well. Because, after all, this was "child abduction" at its highest degree.[9] Then Canada would not only have to answer to us but to the rest of the world with embarrassment and humiliation. It was definitely a "black eye" in the history of Canada. Of course, this was only a "bluff" I made, because at that time, even though I did not have the resources to do what I said I wanted to do, this might work in our favour.[10]

I instructed our lawyer to tell Canada's lawyers what I was threatening to do. Shortly after that, Canada did come forward and admitted that they had done us wrong and that they owed something for what they have done to us. I must keep in mind that by this time, while I was travelling and spreading the word, making loud noises about how Canada had tried to destroy us, other groups of people were doing a lot of quiet work. It seemed like we had sparked a light in everybody's mind across the country; by this time people knew that Canada had done us wrong and owed us something and that they must make things right for the Indian Survivors across this wonderful country we call Canada.

Canada already had their team of lawyers (approximately twelve of them) strategizing on how to avoid dealing with the Survivors of Indian residential schools of Canada. They tried to justify what Canada had done to us was okay in those days, and that all they wanted to do was give us a better life and at the same time educate us.[11] To me this was a deceitful manner in which they (Canada) tried to make it look like what they wanted to do for us was to give us a better way of life. They wanted to educate us at the same time. What they really wanted to do was to make us into something completely different. They wanted us to be absorbed into their white culture. I think that was a very ignorant way to say that our culture was not good enough for us and that their culture was better than ours.

By this time, many people and organizations were getting involved to help bring about justice and compensation for the residential school Survivors of Canada. I firmly believe that our efforts were still leading the way, because when our lawyer stated that we could not sue the government, we kept on fighting. I firmly believe that it was our group that had to deal with many issues, such as when Canada admitted that they did us wrong, they tried to apply a statute of limitations on us. I think that this was just a tactic and a stumbling block to discourage us so that we would not continue our lobbying for justice and compensation. Such a statute would "lessen" Canada's obligations to pay the required financial payments to Survivors, virtually wiping out 75 to 80 percent of them. If that was upheld (the statute of limitations) most of the agreements with Survivors would have been wiped out. This is what these delay tactics and processes were all about.[12]

At the same time, there were many people and First Nations organizations beginning to get involved. I began to think that we, the Manitoba Indian Residential School Survivors Movement and our Survivors needed to consider doing things in a "traditional way." So, we went to our Elder, the late Dave Murdock, who was living at the time, to give us a "traditional name."

I took tobacco and gave it to him, and I explained that I wanted to do this a little differently by taking on a traditional name. He explained to me that he had to meditate on it and think about it and that he had to go to the woods for seven days and that he will try to return with a name for us. Seven days later, he came back with the name of "Spirit Wind" (translated into English), given to him by the great spirits.

We asked him what the name meant, and he explained it this way: "If you can imagine yourself walking in the wilderness, and all of a sudden a whirl wind of snow, it could be dust, leaves, grass blowing around you in a spiral motion. This is our spirits blowing around us as we walk in the wilderness. It explains that our work, our desires and aspirations are in the spirit of the winds." I was taken in by his interpretation as I had experienced that type of whirl in the school, while I was running away, when I was drunk on the streets, and even today. That is your spirit that you carry with you wherever life takes you and will follow you into the grave. Those powerful words have guided our mission to help residential school, day school, Sixties Scoop, and other Survivors who have been left out of official agreements as the wind still follows them. We asked if it would be okay to add MB or Manitoba to the name. He said that this was okay and this name is for all Survivors of Canada as each person has their own story or spirit which has guided them through this dark period in our history.[13]

In January of 2003, we officially adopted the name of "Spirit Wind." We held our first official inaugural meeting at the Winnipeg Indian and Métis Friendship Centre on 14 February 2003. This was the official beginning of Spirit Wind, and since then, every meeting, discussion, decision, and action was conducted under this name.

Exactly a month later on 14 March 2003, we held a successful meeting with northwestern Ontario First Nations, who were originally under our Treaty #1 in Manitoba, in Eagle River. We had over 250 people attend including several chiefs and even three grand chiefs. We received overwhelming support and we realized that we would need support from national leadership.

Things began to look much better as numerous lawsuits had been started as more Survivors began speaking out. Spirit Wind managed to gain moral support from our local and national leadership, indicating support from our provincial representatives, the Assembly of Manitoba

Chiefs (AMC) and from our national representatives, the Assembly of First Nations (AFN) (Appendix C, D, and E).

As we gained support in 2003, we formalized a strategy plan that laid out our intentions with Spirit Wind. We clearly stated that we were "frustrated with the inaction of the Government of Canada, and their strategy and tactics to control the process without fair and accepted input from Residential School Survivors and their legal counsel."[14] We demanded that the government provide "fair, just, and timely compensation for the abuse and cultural genocide suffered by those who attended the Canadian Indian Residential School System."[15] I also told the chiefs that we had other provinces such as Saskatchewan, Ontario, and Alberta who had contacted Spirit Wind in hopes of establishing similar Survivor associations. Moreover, we explained that our ultimate goal was to "have a network of Residential School Survivor associations across the country to pressure the government and advocate strongly to ensure fair and just treatment for all Survivors across Canada."[16]

It seemed we were finally making some progress, and wherever we went, we got support for our efforts as people recognized something was brewing. In 2004, our membership continued to rise as more pressure was applied to the federal government. At this time, our organization was representing over 5,000 residential school Survivors across Manitoba, and Canada.[17] At the time, Canada was already privately settling an estimated 12,000 claims of abuse or roughly 15 percent of the number of residential school Survivors through a $1.7 billion settlement plan. Our people were divided again among those who could afford legal representation and those who were still trying to get their life back in order after the severe abuses in the schools. During this period approximately 1,250 Survivors were compensated with $71 million, but a clause stated that they could never sue the federal government again for language loss or cultural abuses.

We believed this divided our efforts in seeking compensation as each case would require individual lawyers who would also seek individual fees. In addition, the federal government only had to pay 70 percent of proven damages for sexual and physical abuse while the remaining 30 percent were neglected.[18] I was interviewed by the Globe and Mail and said, "the government should realize we were all in it together ... why does the Canadian government have to take us to court to see what they've done to us?"[19] Was this real justice? Or an attempt to divide and conqueror our peoples' rising efforts similar to what they had done when they took our lands, made the schools, and created this judicial mechanism. During this exact same time, for instance, Canada was still fighting a legal battle in British Columbia which demanded that they pay for 100 percent of the damages inflicted by residential schools.[20]

However, a lawyer named Darcy Merkur, from the firm Thompson Rogers, was starting to organize a national class-action lawsuit that would provide compensation for all Survivors of the residential schools under one ruling. This would prevent individual lawyers from taking a significant portion of settlements and allow Canada to be sued with all Survivors involved. He explained that "we're saying that's not fair ... this was institutional child abuse. They were basically scarred for life."[21] Merkur's firm supported the Baxter National Class Action which would cover all residential school Survivors since 1920. Spirit Wind's involvement in this case will be explained in the next few pages as I try to unpack the complicated procedures that would follow.

We applied for a grant from Canada and we were surprised to receive a small grant of $50,000 the first year to help with our operation, so that we could now have our travel paid for when we held meetings; it was also used to help pay for administrative procedures. We had to get the South East Resource Development Council (SERDC) to sponsor Spirit Wind because we were not incorporated at the time.

SERDC appointed a co-ordinator of our organization who began to schedule our meetings, took minutes, paid the board members' honorariums and travel expenses, looked after the financial accounts, and wrote reports for funding purposes. We sure appreciated all the work he did for Spirit Wind. I personally think he did a fantastic job like no other. Plus, the South East Resource Development Council was very generous and helped out in any way they could. The following year, the second and final time we ever received federal funding for our organization, we received $25,000.00. Now, SERDC could start on our work.[22]

Our board of directors of Spirit Wind decided, after the persistence of one or more of the directors, that we would move our office to Long Plain First Nation under the sponsorship of Arrowhead Development Corporation at the old residential school in Portage la Prairie, Manitoba. We really appreciated all the support that Long Plain First Nation had given Spirit Wind; in fact, they contributed approximately $15,000.00 to our cause, along with free rent from their organization, Arrowhead Development Corporation. Long Plain's support and those two government grants were the only external funding Spirit Wind ever received.

Around this time, I strongly believed that we needed to have a national voice to help succeed in our cause. As it so happened in 2003/04, I received a call from a gentleman, Mr Mike Cachagee, who was living in Sault Ste Marie, Ontario, at the time. It was like another "God-sent gift" because it came about when I was thinking about setting up a national organization to be our voice and speak for us on a national basis. It would complement exactly what Spirit Wind was doing provincially. The organization wanted to follow a similar model that I had outlined in my Spirit Wind presentations.

When Mr Cachagee called me, he said that he had heard that I was involved in working towards getting a settlement for abuses we suffered in the residential schools with an organization called Spirit wind. I said, "Yes I am, and I am still chairperson of the organization." He then asked if I would be interested setting up a national organization to speak and work on behalf of IRS Survivors across Canada. He said that he had been working on this project for some time, that he had people willing to represent the other provinces of Canada, and that I could represent Manitoba. I immediately and very gladly accepted this opportunity. I told him that this was exactly what I had hoped would happen because we needed a strong, national voice to speak and to represent us nationally.

It wasn't long before we had our first National Indian Residential School Survivors meeting. We voted on and accepted a proposal to name our organization the National Indian Residential School Survivors Society of Canada and to locate the head office in Sault Ste Marie. We had representation from every province and territory across Canada. What a blessing this was. At first, I was a regular board member, and later on I was the secretary-treasurer for about a year and a half. The last three years I was chairperson of our national organization. Today, the organization no longer exists, because funding for this operation stopped. It was good but also a sad memory. I met so many good people and made so many good friends from across all of Canada.

I was so happy that we, the Survivors of Canada, now had a national voice to represent us. We travelled across Canada promoting the IRSS cause for justice and compensation. The churches, like the Anglican, the

United Church, the Presbyterian Church, the Mennonite Churches of Canada, etc., all got involved, with the exception of the Roman Catholic Church, for some reason we could not really figure out. At the same time, during all of the time, I was still chairperson of Spirit Wind. We were finally being heard.

The process to a resolution of claims was a very complicated process that will require some explaining about the legal tactics Canada used. The first compensation package was called the Alternative Dispute Resolution (ADR) process, which was established in November of 2003.[23] This resolution was intended to help solve the numerous Indian residential school disputes, without ever going to court.[24] Spirit Wind did not accept Canada's offer and attempts to resolve the IRSS abusive legacies because it only compensated the sexually and physically abused. I said that it was not worth the paper that it was written on as it did not include all the abuses. The ADR process did not recognize and address other abuses, such as emotional abuse, loneliness, and psychological abuse; student-on-student abuse; loss of parenting opportunities; and loss of language and cultural identity.[25]

In May 2003, I had already explained that "The current Alternative Dispute Resolution Process (ADR) as mentioned earlier, is unsatisfactory and only deals with sexual and severe physical abuse, as these are the only categories of abuse that the Government of Canada will recognize to date. Spirit Wind has passed a resolution in support of the national class action lawsuit on behalf of Survivors across Canada for compensation for sexual, physical, psychological/emotional, cultural, and language abuse."[26]

Moreover, once an ADR was resolved, the plaintiff could no longer sue the federal government or take any other action such as joining any of the remaining class action lawsuits. Several members of Spirit Wind were negatively affected by this resolution and we never supported the compensation settlement agreement. The Truth and Reconciliation Legacy Report adequately described the ADR story of one of the founding members of Spirit Wind, Mrs Flora Merrick.[27]

It was very difficult to solicit donations and funding from any organization, corporation, or individuals because when potential donors found out that we were in the process of suing the Government of Canada many got cold feet and backed off for fear of retribution from the Government of Canada. In fact, this was one of the main reasons, we feel, why we have not been able to get charitable status from the government even to this date. However, this has not stopped our drive to continue our struggle to succeed. As you can see, there were many things happening almost at the same time.

It wasn't long before our lawyer, Dennis Troniak, asked if I would be willing to go make a presentation in the House of Commons to the Aboriginal Standing Committee. On 17 February 2005, a delegation from Spirit Wind accompanied by our lawyer, Dennis Troniak, travelled to Ottawa: myself, one of my colleagues, Ruth Roulette (Spirit Wind committee member), her late mother, Ms Grace Daniels, and her late grandmother, Ms Flora Merrick. These three ladies all went to the same residential school and suffered the same kind of abuses. They were very ready to tell their stories and their experiences of abuse. They were allowed to speak in their Native tongue, which was Dakota Sioux, and Ruth Roulette interpreted. This was quite an emotional presentation that day. Dennis Troniak opened the presentations with his remarks and then I gave my presentation (Appendix F). Then, Ruth's grandmother gave her testimony in Dakota Sioux, as did Ruth's mother. In between her mother and grandmother, Ruth testified in English.

In my presentation, I spoke of several concerns and issues of Spirit Wind and the work we were trying to accomplish for the Indian Residential School Survivors of Canada, and what Canada should be doing to help to resolve IRSS abuse issues. I mentioned that Spirit Wind is totally independent and that we are a grassroots voice for residential school Survivors. As will be discussed in this chapter, we did not support or welcome the Alternative Dispute Resolution process but rather, we strongly supported the Baxter national class action as an option to deal with the residential school claims. I also stated that I had recently signed a memorandum of understanding (MOU) pledging our support for this national class action.[28] During the recent certification of the Ontario Mohawk class actions through the Cloud Action decision of the Ontario Court of Appeal, I was advised that this was to set the precedent for national class actions. These comments were particularly useful to the House of Commons as they were deciding on a number of different resolutions for Survivors' claims. I will explain how this process was not aligned with the intentions of Spirit Wind members.

You see this is how it works: before there is any financial compensation realized, it must be rendered or directed by a court order/decision before any public funds are distributed. Before a court order in rendered, it must be "certified" before the case goes to a trial, meaning that when the court deliberates a legal decision it will have facts and considerations in place. This is the process that must happen before any legal court order is rendered in a court of law.

Grace Daniels, another founding member of Spirit Wind, was the stepdaughter of Flora Merrick, noted above. She was also brought to the House of Commons where she publicly explained her story and the massive issues with the ADR process. Her daughter, Ruth Roulette, translated to the House:

> I would not let them break my spirit. Those strappings were done in front of other children, which also made me feel degraded and humiliated. I felt degraded and humiliated. I received numerous other strappings and beatings that would at times last for several minutes and up to a half hour, but I would not give in. I would not let them break my spirit. Those strappings were done in front of other children, which also made me feel degraded and humiliated ... I was also punished and threatened when I tried to speak my native Ojibway language. Often, I was hungry, denied food as punishment; and the food was often bland, like slop ... The fact that I was slotted into the model B category of the ADR process and only entitled to a maximum amount of $3,500 for my pain and suffering, to me, is a great injustice. I was offered only $3,000, which I turned down as a slap in the face ...I feel that I was revictimized by an uncaring and an unsympathetic government process that was only interested in denying justice at whatever cost. I have been told that the federal government probably spent close to $20,000 to verify and hold my hearing. All the costs my lawyer and I incurred I believe are not covered because I turned down the ADR settlement process offer.[29]

Grace was victimized again by the Canadian government as they did not provide her with a fair process despite making her go through the entire procedure of bringing up her trauma. After her brave speech in the

House of Commons she denied her $3,000 payment and joined the Baxter Class Action lawsuit, which would lead to the Indian Residential School Settlement Agreement. She kept her resilient spirit, stating that "the ADR does not reflect the suffering we underwent as prisoners of the system."[30] Sadly, Grace passed away in 2015, but was a dear friend of mine as we both attended Portage la Prairie Residential School.[31]

That February, in 2005, after our speech to the House of Commons, the Standing Committee of Aboriginal Affairs and Northern Development agree to try and settle all cases of former students replacing the early notion of those "victimized by pedophiles."[32] However, when Canada admitted that they had done us wrong, it seemed that if we wanted something that was rightfully ours, they would not budge or give until they (the Government of Canada) were taken to a court of law. I think the reason for this is the fact that Canada knew we were old and poor people, and court cases take a long time to resolve and it costs a lot of money that our people have difficulty obtaining.

A 2003–04 report found that the government was only providing $4.8 million to Survivors with another $68.3 million for the operating expenditures of the settlement, with over a third going to the Department of Justice lawyers who were defending Canada.[33] For instance, the Assembly of First Nations chief, Phil Fontaine, was particularly angry over the costs and time taken to come to a fair agreement: "Canada can continue to litigate. It can continue to pay huge court costs and hundreds of millions in legal fees while maintaining an adversarial relationship with the First Nations. Or it can act honourably. The government, he said, should do the right thing and the quick thing; an estimated five Survivors die each day. There [were] once 50,000 former students, he said, but many have died over the years without justice and reconciliation – 20,000 since 1991. The rest of us are still waiting."[34]

This way, they hoped that the issues would "fade away" and never be dealt with or resolved. This we feel is another way of Canada creating "stalling tactics," which they are very good at. I repeated these comments in April of 2005 to NOW Magazine, stating that their approach was "seriously flawed and deliberately attempts to avoid responsibility and limit liability. They must be waiting until all of us are dead."[35]

Canada pulled off a deceitful, shady, crooked, and shameful process, what they called "The Manitoba Indian Residential School Pilot Project."

This process was set by the Government of Canada to take in as many Survivors as they possibly could get in such a short time. It was carried out just in conjunction when the ADR process came into existence. I was so angry when I found out what had really happened. Canada set up somewhere in or near Dauphin, Manitoba, close to Skageeng First Nation, and asked that all lawyers in Manitoba and from other provinces who had IRS Survivors as clients to be in attendance to make a quick and discrete deal.[36]

It was very sad how the Survivors were "sucked into" accepting a "take it or leave it" offer. Elderly people were offered from as little as $5,000 to a maximum of $10,000 for the abuses they suffered in IRS Schools. They were made to sign a "waiver," where they agreed to never come back and sue Canada again for their abuses. What a shame to Canada, once again, for what they pulled off on these poor, elderly people. As far as I am concerned, this is still another "black eye" in the history of Canada.

I must thank and commend our lawyer, Dennis Troniak, for pulling out of this scam that Canada was attempting. Mr Troniak pulled out because he did not like what Canada was doing to the Survivors, especially the elderly. He did not want to subject his clients to this process; he said it was like leading "lambs to slaughter" and he did not want to be a part of that whatsoever. Hats off to this gentleman, who showed that he was all heart and that he was not only interested in money matters.[37]

These elderly people did not understand what they were signing. They put their faith in their lawyers, whose duty was to protect them. More than fifty people signed away their right to sue Canada for further damages. All they were given was a small, one-time, compensation ($5,000–10,000) and only a few minutes to testify to their ordeals and experiences in these IRS Schools. When they tried to continue, beyond their two or three minutes, they were cut off and told to "sign here," take this because this is all you will ever receive. These poor people accepted this as compensation, not realizing that just around the corner another compensation package was about to happen.[38]

This is why we spoke very loudly against the ADR process, and would not acknowledge it. Our lawyer, Dennis Troniak, asked us to let this process stand for now, it was something that we never had before and we (could) continue to work for something better. He said it is something for now, and we can work at it and hopefully changes can be made down the way. At the time, I refused to have anything to do with what our lawyer had decided, but in the end, I supported him. I personally did not accept any part of it.[39]

As time elapsed, and around about that time, there were other class action law suits underway. We heard of the Blackwater case in Calgary and the Cloud and Baxter cases in Ontario.[40] A lawyer named Darcy Merkur, from the firm Thompson Rogers, was starting to organize a national class-action lawsuit that would provide compensation for all Survivors of the residential school system under one ruling. This would prevent individual lawyers from taking a significant portion of settlements and allow Canada to be sued with all Survivors involved. He explained that "we're saying that's not fair … this was institutional child abuse. They were basically scarred for life."[41] Merkur's firm supported the Baxter National Class Action which would cover all residential school Survivors since 1920.[42] Spirit Wind's involvement in this case will be explained in the next few pages as I try and unpack the complicated procedures that follow.

I read, heard, and inquired about the Baxter case in Ontario. I learned about the case and believed that if Spirit Wind would help and support the Baxter brothers in their case, it would open the doors to including all of the other abuses I had previously mentioned, such as other sexual abuses, other physical abuses, student-on-student abuses, bullying, psychological and mental abuse, loss of parenting opportunities, and loss of opportunities for compensation. I told our lawyer that we would be supporting the Baxter class action and asked him to let the people who were working on resolving that court case know what our intentions were.

I would like to explain as much as I can about the many court cases that were occurring in the mid 1990s until the early 2000s. For example, there were maybe as many as ten to twelve class actions against Canada that could all be for justice and financial compensation for the Indian Residential School Survivors. What the federal courts of Canada would do is make a "short list" of the strongest, most complete class action suits that had the most members attached to them. Then, it would decide which of these cases would represent and satisfy all the rest of the smaller classes sitting before them. They would "certify" one that would address all issues and classes. At this point, it was the Cloud Class Action and the Baxter Class Action cases that were being considered for certification.[43]

It is my understanding that our support of the Baxter class action helped put the Cloud Case through that ultimately brought the IRSSA about.[44]

I feel that the Aboriginal Standing Committee certainly had something to do with all that took place. Before we left the House of Commons, we were promised that something would definitely be done to help us resolve our issues. The Aboriginal Standing Committee all unanimously agreed to help and to do something in support of Spirit Wind's cause.

Shortly after we finished our presentations in the House of Commons, while we were still in the hallway, our lawyer's phone started to ring. It was a representative from the Senate asking if we would go over there and give them a report of what we had just completed in the House committee. Of course, we all agreed to go and repeat our presentations. I was then invited to Rideau Hall in front of the governor general, Michaëlle Jean, to give another informative talk about my experiences in residential schools. She also supported our goals.

About three weeks after arriving home from the Ottawa trip, I received a phone call from the national consortium lawyer's chairperson, Mr Darcy Merkur of Toronto. He asked if I was still chairperson of Spirit Wind, and if so, would I give them a letter of support (the memorandum of understanding I mentioned previously) because they were going to trial for the Baxter case.[45] I was more than happy to accommodate him and his team of lawyers and that I would personally hand deliver the letter to him in Sault Ste Marie, Ontario. My wife and I drove and made a trip out of it. We went by vehicle driving from north of Winnipeg during the winter months, January of 2005. We drove east on the Trans-Canada Highway.[46]

I did not realize the danger in driving east on the Trans-Canada during the winter months. The snow was very high and the road was very narrow and very slippery in most places. The highway was narrow because of the build-up of ploughed snow pushed high as there was no other place to push the snow but upwards.

I remember driving along those roads because it was storming and blowing with drifting snow and it was very cold. I thought I was seeing things when we almost hit a moose. It was actually standing on the side of the road on the drift, looking down on us. We actually hit his nose on the passenger side of the windshield. I often tease my wife about the fact that a moose almost kissed her. It frightened both of us, because it startled her so much and it happened so very quickly. I must say that this was a very dangerous drive, and I was beginning to get very tired when we finally arrived at our destination.

We finally made it safely to Sault St Marie to deliver Spirit Wind's memorandum of understanding to Darcy Merkur.[47] I remember this whole episode very clearly because I got very sick with the flu. I had left my wife waiting for me and resting at the hotel room we were staying in. I got so sick I drove myself to the local hospital. I was very weak, I almost passed out. I barely made it to the hospital. I hadn't mentioned a thing to anyone at the meeting, that I didn't feel very well or that I was heading for the local hospital.

When I arrived at the hospital, I tried to register, and I think I passed out and fell to the floor. Next thing I knew, I woke up, hooked up to all sorts of tubes and breathing apparatus. I did not realize that I had had a heart attack and that I had been out for a few hours.

Meanwhile, during all of this commotion, my wife was waiting for me at the hotel. I was well past my due time to arrive back to the room. When I finally realized that my wife was waiting for me at the hotel, I called the head nurse and told her that my wife was probably worried sick about me by that time.

My wife did not know anything about the town of Sault Ste Marie. She did not know that I had had a heart attack and I was very sick in the hospital. When I told my nurse about her, I could not even remember the name of our hotel. I was very worried about my wife. After calling a number of hotels in town, the nurse finally found my wife. I can't imagine what was going through her mind because she did not know which hospital I was in. Eventually, she was able to find where I was and we were together again.[48]

I am telling this story because it is very important to tell the people some of the things that had to happen in order to help bring about the Indian Residential School Survivors Agreement for compensation. I had to deliver this MOU and put it in the hands of the right lawyer, Mr Merkur, because without it, our lawyers would have had a more difficult time in court. It helped them end their case as the lawyers had to show that they had Aboriginal support during their fight for our justice.[49] The numerous lawsuits that were started and won by Indigenous people around the country were absorbed and settled in the eventual Indian Residential School Agreement.[50] Our hopes and dreams of finally being recognized were becoming true.

I believe that Spirit Wind, the National Consortium of Residential School Survivors' Counsel, the Cloud and Baxter class actions were the appropriate forum and vehicle for a broad, national, and negotiated settlement on behalf of all residential school Survivors of Canada. More-over, the Baxter case would permit all Indigenous people in the country who attended school after 1920 who were abused to receive compensa-tion.[51] This is why we so strongly supported the Baxter class action.

We also strongly believe that at the time the Cloud class action was being considered for certification, the Baxter case would have been certi-fied if the Cloud case was not going to be certified. The courts of Canada knew that if the Cloud case did not make it, the Baxter case would as they repeatedly tried to slow down the class action's movement. So, without this lawsuit and several others across the country, the government could have kept delaying our efforts until we had stopped our work.[52] The even-tual certification of the Cloud Case also proved to Canada that these types of cases could win and force them to the bargaining table.

As you can see, everyone, whatever their efforts were, big or small, had a part in bringing about the Indian Residential School Survivors' Agree-ment. I strongly believe that had it not been for the commitment and dogged persistence of Spirit Wind and the grassroots support we received which led to the Aboriginal Standing Committee on 17 February 2005, in the House of Commons, there would have been no victory for the Surviv-ors of Canada. However, it was done and we all had a part in the success of this bigger victory.

The Baxter class action lawsuit was never heard. Rather, it was settled with the help of Darcy Merkur and the National Consortium, as it was merged under the "Fontaine v. Canada" ruling. This ruling led to the Indian Residential School Settlement Agreement.[53] Merkur would later explain these developments to me in 2016.[54]

At the time of the agreement, however, I was not that thrilled about the price per year given to residential school Survivors nor the consul-tations that took place with grassroots Survivors. The words of Grace Daniels and other Survivors echoed in my mind as she felt that it was a "slap in the face" to only receive $3,000 compensation for her time in the residential school. Granted, Survivors would receive $10,000 up front, but only another $3,000 per year of school attendance seemed especially low for students. Over time, I would have more complaints about the Indian Residential School Agreement as I believe our voice became lost as soon as the legal system and AFN took over the proceedings.[55] In 2005, before the official agreement was even signed, I told Windspeaker Publication, "We're not in total agreement with the ten and three [$10,000 lump sum, plus $3,000 per year in the schools] because each claim is different. A lot of our Elders here in Manitoba are extremely upset with the 10 and 3. That's simply because there were no grassroots people having any input in the process.[56] Our members wanted a much larger number and I told the publication in 2005 that what we're recommending is a formula of $25,000 [lump sum payment] plus $10,000 [for each year in the schools]. We think [Justice Frank] Iacobucci (who negotiated the Indian Residential School Settlement Agreement) should work between those two numbers."[57]

Once the Canadian legal system fully took over the process of "calculating" the damages done by Canada, even more issues were created over who was correct in their story.[58]

It has taken some time to gather testimonies of other Survivors who went through the process, but many of them feel their concerns were not adequately heard. After I, and numerous other Survivors who were a part of Spirit Wind, underwent our Independent Assessment Process we found that it was very unforgiving for our Elders.[59] Coupled with the modest common experience payments and a few lawyers who began to rip off the elderly, I have decided to show how the agreement was not 100 percent perfect in its implementation.[60]

After the agreement was signed, I would receive phone calls from other Survivors in Manitoba who were devastated over the amounts that lawyers were taking after their individual settlements were reached. It was not until 2011 that a federal system of checks and balances caught a lawyer in Winnipeg who overcharged twenty-six Survivors nearly $400,000. I told the Winnipeg Free Press that "I'm glad the service is there for the people ... [but] it's a shame someone would try to do this because you're taking advantage of the poorest of the poor."[61] I realized that this would continue to occur for some Survivors, which added to the already painful experience of recounting their experiences. It would take time before these Survivors received their money as the lawyer had invested in real estate property in Israel.[62] We were glad this lawyer was caught, but we wondered how many others had quickly taken the money without ever being caught. In addition, Survivors continued to be concerned regarding the outcomes for their abusers.

Throughout the Independent Assessment Process, Survivors' testimonies would reveal some of the darkest crimes in Canada's history with the names of abusers clearly revealed. Since the victims were required to demonstrate proof of what occurred, and blamed if they could not, cor-roborated leads should have resulted in criminal prosecutions.[63] The In-dependent Assessment Process allowed that "The Government of Canada will attempt to locate and contact alleged perpetrators. If an alleged perpe-trator is found and wants to participate, the alleged perpetrator must pro-vide a witness statement and agree to appear at his/her hearing to provide oral testimony."[64]

Therefore, abusers were "invited" to provide testimony, but they had even more protection from criminal prosecution as they had the right to "choose not to participate." In this case, "An alleged perpetrator may choose not to participate. The alleged perpetrator may also choose not to be advised of the claimant's name or the allegations against them. An alleged perpetrator is entitled to participate by submitting a written state-ment in response to the allegations, and by attending his/her hearing."[65] The IAP website also makes it clear that participation in this process would not result in criminal charges, indicating, "The IAP is separate from any criminal proceedings. The IAP is a compensation process for cases of abuse at Indian Residential Schools, not a criminal process (see my own Appendix B). The IAP uses the civil burden of proof, called a "balance of probabilities," not the criminal standard of proof required for prosecution in a court of law.[66]

Thus, in 2013, when I was asked by CBC News regarding the govern-ment's new plan to hire "private investigators" in order to find some of the alleged perpetrators, I said explicitly that, "I think the whole exercise is useless. It's a waste of money. If you go to court and you're found guilty, you go to jail. And that's what should happen to them."[67] I and numerous other Spirit Wind Survivors had undergone the IAP process, identified the abusers, and knew the rules protecting the alleged perpetrators from being criminally charged.

What was the point of spending money out of the agreement in order to ask alleged perpetrators if they wanted to write a statement, but not be criminally charged? This fact of the agreement has continued to be a sore spot for Survivors, especially when numerous testimonies identified the same abusers providing plenty of ammunition for criminal investiga-tions.[68] Our fight was far from over though, as other Survivors voices still needed to be heard.

7   INDIAN DAY SCHOOLS

I will attempt to describe what a "day school" is. Indian day schools were schools built and funded by the Federal Department of Indian Affairs, and which Aboriginal students across Canada were required to attend by law according to the Indian Act. Unlike Indian residential schools, Aboriginal students did not reside at Indian day schools. Only in very few circumstances (seasonal, weather conditions, etc.) would a student reside at an Indian day school. Indian day schools include those day schools that operated both on and off reserves. Churches were very much involved in Indian day schools. In most cases, Indian day schools were operated and maintained by the same religious organizations that administered Indian residential schools. This included Roman Catholic, Anglican, Methodist, and Presbyterian denominations. Although some day school students got to go home at the end of each class day, abuses still occurred.[1]

The abuses in day schools were very similar to those perpetrated in residential schools; don't forget that sexual abuse can happen in seconds. I have had the opportunity to speak to former day school Survivors from my community, Peguis First Nation, and also from Fort Alexander First Nation, Manitoba. All the abuses they spoke about were very similar.[2] Also, I was a day school Survivor of nearly two years and did experience most of the abuses I am speaking about.

There were other abuses I experienced myself, such as pulling of the hair, student-on-student abuses, bullying, strapping, and being ostracized or made to stand up in front of the class with your hands behind your back and balancing a book on your head. Also, I had to write one hundred lines on the class blackboard, saying, "I will never speak Indian again." This was all because I could not speak English, which made it very difficult for me to do. I still remember my teacher's name to this day.[3]

When any of us children complained to our parents about these abuses that were happening to us in these day schools, our parents could not come check and to see if that was really happening because Canada had put an invisible circumference of approximately 100 yards around the day school where they could not enter. If they went within that boundary, they would be charged for trespassing.

When our national leader of the day, Phil Fontaine, was considering accepting the Indian Residential School Agreement, I tried to persuade him to hold off until the "deceased former day school Survivors," the "second generation, the children of Survivors," and "day school Survivors" were considered included in the agreement. He promised he would help us get another settlement/agreement for our people (day school Survivors). Fontaine has supported our initial efforts, but was soon replaced by a different national chief.[4]

When we realized that day school Survivors were not going to be part of the official settlement agreement, we began organizing another attempt at justice. This would take several meetings and the organization of Spirit Wind, but in March of 2009 we were having a meeting on what to do about day school Survivors. It just so happened Joan Jack came by. We knew she was a lawyer, so we asked her if she could help us and if she would be our lawyer to assist us in filing a day school class action against Canada. When we asked her to be our lawyer, she immediately stated that she was not a class action lawyer, but she certainly would help us find one and that she would work with them on our behalf.

We got to work immediately. Joan Jack had her staff set up to take all potential day school Survivors and register them, their schools, their type of abuses, and other details. A database was set up and each Survivor who called was added to it. Their school was researched to determine if in fact they were day schools within the meaning of the Indian Act.

At the same time, Joan and her associates started to develop the statement of claim for the class action. Although Joan had stated she was not a class action lawyer, her belief in our cause and her Indigenous heritage led her to agree to help our case pro bono until a larger firm could take over. We decided that we would do things differently from the way the Indian Residential School Settlement Agreement was created and negotiated. We said that we were not going to lose control of this action this time around, we were going to do it our way, the traditional way. The Indian way of doing things. We did not want the help of the Assembly of First Nations (AFN), the national political leadership of First Nation people and chiefs of Canada. Nor did we want any other organization to "step in" and take over the class action without our permission. As far as I am concerned, the AFN does not represent the grassroots people, the day school Survivors. AFN is accountable to the chiefs of Canada, and the chiefs are accountable to their local representatives of their community, and that's it.[5] We still respect their leadership, however, and sought a 2009 resolution from the Assembly of Manitoba Chiefs which would provide attention to our cause.[6]

I told Joan that once she had completed the first draft of the statement of claim, we were going involve the grassroots people, right from the beginning. We decided that we would take the first draft to Fort Alexander First Nation, near Pine Falls, Manitoba and have the day school Survivors from that community participate in the actual drafting up of the statement of claim. We chose this community because it has a large number of day school Survivors and it was fairly close to our location.

We arranged to go to the community, and we were greeted by hundreds of Survivors, approximately 400 to 500 of them. Joan and her colleagues and staff flashed paragraphs and statements on a big screen on a wall and asked the people what they thought of the sentences, should they be changed or deleted from the statement altogether. I'd never seen so many people who really appreciated what we were doing with and for them. We spent a whole day working on the statement of claim. At the end of day, Joan Jack explained that she and her staff would take this work back to her office, make the changes to the statement according to their suggestions, and come back in a couple of weeks to review the statement. This made the Survivors feel very positive about the process; they felt that they were definitely a part of the class action.

The second time we went to the community, there were approximately 700 plus Survivors that attended the workshop. Our lawyer let them participate by letting them read, edit, and suggest changes to the document. Many of them were very glad that we did this process with them. Then we took the work that was done and wrote a final draft.

The reason why we allowed actual day school Survivors' participation in the drafting of the statement is because we felt that if they were allowed, they can say that they are a part of the claim and that they can take ownership of it. It makes everyone have a vote in the process and able to feel closure after playing a key role in the development of the claim, as it should be. We began spreading the word with the help of other Survivors who had been left out of the Indian Residential School Agreement and suffered the same amount of abuse. In 2011, Joan Jack travelled to the Chiefs of Ontario, Assembly of Manitoba Chiefs, Grand Council of Treaty 3, BC First Nations summit, and general assembly to provide updates about the large database we were compiling.

After the final drafting of the claim, we took the statement into a sweat, and had it blessed at Petersfield, Manitoba.[7] An Elder from Berens River, Manitoba performed the traditional ceremonies. Now, we were set and ready to actually file the statement of claim in a federal court of law in Winnipeg, Manitoba.

A short while after the class action was filed, we changed the name to the Garry McLean National Day School Class Action. The reason for the change was because we felt that it would be appropriate to have a genuine day school Survivor to represent all Survivors. As the plaintiff, I had only spent less than two years at Peguis Day School #3 while Garry was sent at the age of seven until eighteen to Dog Creek Indian Day School. He also had experience working with various political leaders and was informed about the numerous difficulties that this case would have.[8] In 2009, we were both interviewed by CTV where we explained why we wanted to recognize day school Survivors. We believed that Indigenous children in these schools suffered the same types of abuses and would also demonstrate the same intergenerational effects of residential school students, which drove them into drug addiction, incarceration, and suicide. I told the press, "the only difference is they got to go home at the end of the day … it only takes five to ten minutes to abuse somebody."[9] I also explained that the official apology by Prime Minister Stephen Harper in 2008 was thus inadequate, stating, "the apology doesn't mean anything to them because it doesn't include them … Until that day comes that everybody is included in getting justice and fair compensation, there will be no rest."[10]

We also changed the name of our organization, Spirit Wind, to Spirit Wind/Canada Inc. to reflect our position as a national organization for all Survivors across Canada and for day school Survivors. During the Annual General Assembly for Manitoba at the end of 2009 a "Continued Support for Spirit Wind" resolution was passed by the Assembly of Manitoba Chiefs. Moreover, they recognized our efforts thus far and provided the added support to get this lawsuit rolling. In the resolutions, they acknowledged and supported our efforts in "addressing the issue of abuse in Day Schools" (Appendix H).

Our lawyer, at this particular time, Joan, kept her staff working on the database, recording, and researching as Survivors called in and registered every day. It is a lot of work to register and research the schools where they attended because records were scattered across the country. At that time, we did not think another full lawsuit was necessary and the day school complaints may be added to the residential school agreement.[11] The schools were to be put in specific day school categories because there are so many different types of day schools. For example, day schools that are in specific communities (Indian reserves) are schools which are privately owned but funded by the federal government paying for the Indigenous students to attend. Other schools such as private day schools were used, but they were church-run day schools such as the Roman Catholic, Mennonite, Anglican, and Presbyterian organizations that had classrooms in the basements of their churches. Other classifications included sanatorium day schools, those where Indigenous students were sent because they had tuberculosis. There were also schools such as those where a residential school was placed within their communities, and students were allowed to take classes there and to go home at the end of the day; these students are classified as day scholars. I hadn't realized how much work it would take, nor how expensive it would be, to compile these cases.

Spirit Wind had to be run on a voluntary basis, but to do what had to be done for the day school Survivors cost money, which we did not have. CTV News correctly published, "Although the group doesn't have a lot of money, Mason says the fight won't stop until the federal government acknowledges [and compensates] the day school [Survivors]."[12] Spirit Wind is registered nationally as a nonprofit organization. We operate on a "voluntary basis" because we don't have any core funding or support from any government or organization in Canada. This makes our job that much harder.

To alleviate some financial stress for our law firm, and to help with the operations, we decided to conduct some sort of fundraising. We tried to raise funds in a couple of ways; one way was by asking participants/ Survivors to donate on a one-time only basis twenty-five dollars each. This was like a "registration fee." It was solely up to them if they chose to donate or not.

We also developed an annual "Two-Day Day School Conference" where we would give updated information and progress reports on the class action. The First Nation communities were asked if they each could sponsor so many Survivors from their community who wanted to come and attend our conferences in Winnipeg. Not that many came to participate because I think it may have been a little too expensive for them.

With the funds raised we had to pay for the venues, lunches, brochures, pamphlets, and guest speakers' travel. We barely broke even in our attempt to raise money. This was a very costly undertaking, but all in all, the people that were there really enjoyed what they heard and went home satisfied.

It is very unfortunate that these events did not raise enough money to support Joan Jack to continue the great work that she was doing for us and for the people. Joan had put everything she had into this cause and for this case because she believed that it had to continue and that we must succeed for the thousands of people who were depending on us to get justice for them and for what we believe they deserve. Joan believed so much in this that she spent all of her financial resources to keep things afloat, even taking out bank loans. She told CTV News before the process began, "whether you went to a school where you slept at night or you went home at night is not relevant to you ending up not being able to speak your language, feeling ashamed of who you are, being abused spiritually."[13] Unfortunately, it was not enough. Joan, sadly, had to withdraw from being our lawyer. This was one of the hardest days that I could have imagined. God bless her soul, she will be remembered and honoured, and will be in our hearts for what she did for the day school Survivors.[14]

Before she left, she did the next best thing she could do for us, and that was not to leave Spirit Wind and all the people she represented without a lawyer. She engaged another law firm from Winnipeg, Manitoba at about the year 2011/12.[15] Once the transfer was completed, we at Spirit Wind held a few meetings at their office. We tried our best to work with them; however, things did not pan out as well as we had wanted. We felt that progress virtually came to a complete stop. We had difficulty in communicating with this firm, though we made many attempts to work with them. This had carried on for about three and a half years, until we decided that we would seek a new legal counsel. We lost a lot of time waiting on our legal counsel to move forward on our file. I believe that the day school class action was not a priority with them.

Finally, after carefully considering our next move, Garry McLean and I decided that we had to try to move forward and make some progress with our work. We decided to solicit for a new law firm and after going online and posting for a new law firm across Canada, our new law firm and legal team was Gowling WLG located in Ottawa, Ontario. It was sometime in April or May of 2016. This law firm is a well respected firm across Canada and internationally. They are very professional, aggressive, and really want to make progress on our case. I am very impressed with their enthusiasm. It seems like they are "full of vigour" and determined to see this cause to a successful end. The two gentlemen that are working with us now are Robert Winogron and Jeremy Bouchard. I know within my heart this is the best thing that could have happened. We see daylight at the end of the tunnel now. Don't get me wrong, there is much work to be done yet, but they advised us that they will not quit until they complete the work as soon as possible. Already, we have had more meetings with these gentlemen in the short time since we engaged them as our legal team. They are a very large, well-respected firm and I am confident in them and believe in them 100 percent.[16]

Our time with this law firm was not a loss. We managed to increase our membership by following and attending our chiefs' conferences and attending the TRC events throughout Canada. We managed to keep up people's interest and publicize our goals and the day school issues. We gained moral support wherever and whenever we spoke about day school Survivor issues. It is very important that we succeed in obtaining the following:

1   An apology for what they did to us in the Colonial System and the Indian Day School system in the same manner as our brothers and sisters got in the ISSA.
2   Financial compensation for cultural genocide, which is described as trying to make you into another human being (like taking the Indian out of the child), including loss of our language, physical and sexual abuses, emotional trauma/abuse, student on student abuse/bullying.
3   Guarantee that our history must also be incorporated in all public schools, colleges, and universities. This would give non-Native people more insight into what the colonial system has done to our people, our culture and our communities, and how that still affects us every day.

When I first set out on this journey, I said that I would not rest in peace until "all Survivors" of the colonial system get justice for the abuses we encountered during our lifetime. But Canada decided to make things more difficult by dividing us once again. Now, we were separated into residential school Survivors and day school Survivors. How can some suffering be worthier of recognition than others?[17]

Canada knows they did us a grave injustice and terrible wrongs, but they still make things difficult for us by telling us, "if you want compensation, take us to court," knowing that this is a very long and a very costly process. Canada knows that we are destitute, and I suspect they are hoping that it will prove too costly for us to go through the courts or that we will all die or give up and drop the issue. That will never happen. We are a proud and determined people. It is unbelievable how many of our people are passing away. This fight is very urgent. We are working as quickly as possible on this file for them.

I am so determined to work out a solution with Canada. They must come to reason with us and to do the right and honourable thing. I may have to consider other motives to make Canada understand that this is their problem, not ours, and we are here to help them solve their problem. We cannot resolve it without their input.

To date, our law firm is working very hard and is making progress every day. Already they have revised the day school class action because the original statement of claim would have not been accepted, so it had to be re-filed in a federal court of law. We, Spirit Wind representatives and our two lawyers of Gowling WLG, conduct weekly conference call meetings; Garry and I travel anywhere we are summoned to give updates and new information on the file. Just recently, we went to the Enoch Cree Nation, near Edmonton, to give a one-day seminar progress report to the day school Survivors in the area. It was a resounding success; we had approximately 250 to 300 participants-Survivors. We had people come from Saddle Lake First Nation, Alberta, Onion Lake First Nation, Saskatchewan, Fort McMurray, Alberta, and from many other locations. We have been invited to do the same presentation in Fort McMurray in the near future.

Due to circumstances beyond my control, I cannot expose or devolve specific issues dealing with the ongoing process of the Garry McLean Indian Day School Class Action. We hope the agreement will give a voice to the thousands of silent Survivors that have not been able to seek their own truth and justice. Our lead lawyer, Mr Robert Winogron, has been diligently collecting and creating a database of over 14,000 Survivors who attended day schools. We believe the actual number is much higher than 100,000 Survivors but these reports detail the exact same abuses that occurred in the residential schools. He has also visited communities and Survivors throughout the country agreeing that "the only real distinction between the experiences of residential-school students and those of day-school students is that the day-school students went home at night."[18]

On 21 June 2018, Justice Michael Phelan accepted our statement of claim and it was certified in the federal courts. We have accused the federal government of "designing the schools to strip students of their Aboriginal culture and identity and to prevent them from being able to pass their spiritual, cultural, and linguistic heritage onto future generations. It says the government breached the duty of care that it owed to the Indigenous children and operated the institutions in an atmosphere of brutality and intimidation."[19]

It has taken over nine years before the federal government has consented to this type of case and we are optimistic that we may be able to quickly resolve our complaints. A spokesman for Minister of Crown-Indigenous Relations Carolyn Bennett said, "the government of Canada is committed to righting past wrongs, especially those involving Indigenous children, outside of litigation."[20] This process needs to happen right away as more Survivors pass away each day due to the length of time it has taken to be recognized.

Throughout the fall of 2018, discussions between Gowling WLG and the Ministry of Crown-Indigenous Relations regarding our day school class action continued to be negotiated in a manner which would help all survivors without reliving traumatic experiences. On 6 December 2018, I was invited back to the House of Commons for an official announcement by Minister Carolyn Bennett, as the government had reached a settlement in principle with our lawsuit. It is difficult to put the emotions into words, but we were thrilled that all students who attended a colonial education system would receive some type of compensation for the cultural abuses that occurred. In addition, the government finally acknowledged that similar types of abuses that occurred in the residential school system also occurred in the day school system.[21]

However, just a few weeks later, in February 2019, I lost my friend and fellow advocate Garry McLean. I recounted my last conversation with him to the CBC during the final hearing in May of 2019. I said, "What's going to happen if the roof caves in and you leave us? What about the class action?" And he said, "Well Ray, you put me there. You taught me everything. You know what has to be done. Just get it done. Just get it done, bro." As the lawsuit enters the final stages, I hope we can get it done before it's too late

(above) Raymond at House of Commons, 2018. Photo by Jorge Barrera, used with permission.

(below) Raymond on Parliament Hill for Indian Day School Announcement, 2018. Left to Right, Robert Winogron, Garry McLean, Minister of Crown-Indigenous Relations Carolyn Bennett, Raymond Mason, and Jeremy Bouchard. Used with permission of Raymond Mason.

for other survivors to achieve justice.[22] I will not and cannot discuss any other specific action in order to protect what is exactly going on at this time pertaining to the lawsuit. I do not want to jeopardize or to undermine or destroy any working proceedings to this class action. Furthermore, in all the ongoing proceedings, we, Spirit Wind, fully support our legal team.

8 THE TRUTH AND RECONCILIATION EVENTS

As far as I can recall, when I first heard about the Truth and Reconciliation Commission (TRC) component of the Indian Residential School System Agreement, I had mixed feelings. This is mainly because, at first, I did not understand its goals and objectives. Once I understood what it was all about, and that the outcome and findings would be used for educational purposes to help the people outside "Indian Country" understand what happened to us Native people in Canada, I supported it wholeheartedly. It is very important to me that the findings of the TRC be developed and integrated into the Canadian school curricula and into the hearts and minds of the ordinary Canadians who have never heard of the Indian residential school legacy.

My personal interpretation and opinion of the TRC is that we Survivors tell you the truth about all the atrocities that we experienced in the Indian residential schools and the attempts to try to assimilate us into the mainstream of society. We tell you who harmed us and how they harmed us, that we were only children at the time, and it was very easy to hurt us. It was very easy to traumatize and scare the living daylights out of us, make us think and feel worthless and inferior to white society.

I personally did not tell my story or personal experiences of residential schools to the TRC. I am not sure why I did not. I remember trying to help the Elders from my community and other communities get to these gatherings or hearings to tell their personal stories. I remember being very upset because many of the Survivors had to fend entirely for themselves. They had to find a place to sleep, to pay for food and gas, etc. There was no money to cover the Elders' travel expenses. I could not understand this because they said there were no funds to help the Elders but there seemed to be a lot of funds to pay for the entertainers or guest speakers who attended. I was angry about this and I did not participate in the hearing when it was in Winnipeg. I thought it was wrong that only Survivors who had the time or money would have their stories told in these formal settings. At the time, I was also disappointed that significant amounts of money were being directed to these "truth seeking efforts" when the government of the day had said that Canada had "no history of colonialism."[1] I thought these events were political opportunities to finish the story in the manner they wanted without recognizing the thousands of other survivors of the colonial system that had not received any justice.

In my opinion, the colonial system may have succeeded somewhat because some of us Natives did not want to be "Indian" when we came out of that system. We did not want to be Indian for fear of being punished for being who we were. As it turned out, some of us were not even accepted back into our own communities because sometimes they had forgotten who we were. Or we thought that because we had been away for so long we were not the same to be part of them anymore. Sadly, this sometimes even happened in many families.

Have you ever heard of the expression "Not Red enough or White enough"?[2] Well, this is where it came from. After not being accepted back into your own community, and having a hard time being accepted in the white society, you really could not help but feel helpless and feel worthless about yourself. This damaged many people psychologically, including myself.

Consequently, many of us became confused, angry with ourselves, angry at the world, not sure what we were angry about, or why we were so angry. Many of us wanted to be doctors, lawyers, nurses, and teachers. Many of us came out of that system becoming alcoholics and homeless street people. Many of us ended up in trouble with the law, in trouble with our families, fighting with our spouses. Some of us were not accepted by our own families and our own relatives.

This system we experienced made us feel dependent on that very system we came out of, and being in jail kind of reminded many of us of the residential school system. A very regimented system. I for one joined the Canadian Air Force because it reminded me of this system, which was all new for me at the time. Many of us felt more comfortable being incarcerated where we received discipline and room and board.

With the TRC now wrapped up, in my opinion, the Truth has come out, but Reconciliation will only happen if Native people are willing to be humble and to forgive ourselves first, then be willing to forgive others, open to loving one another and working together as a community to survive. Canada and all the people must be willing to do the same with an open mind of understanding and an open heart to realize what we all went through.

Canada must treat and respect Indigenous people as productive assets to this country, not as liabilities. It must live up to the promises it made to us. It must reconcile the lands it has taken from us, and equally share the revenues generated from our resources. I know that if both sides, Canada and the Aboriginal people of this country, do not consider and uphold the promises that came out of the TRC Report, we will never have full reconciliation in this country.[3]

Despite all the efforts, we will have people who will continue to be who they are, racism will continue, people's attitudes towards us will continue to some extent. Native people will continue to struggle for survival because our population is growing so large and so fast that the living needs, such as housing and proper diets, will be very hard to meet as time goes on.

I am very proud of the work the TRC performed. It shows what Native people can accomplish. It proves that we can lead the efforts to resolve our own issues affecting our communities. We understand each other; we know our culture, our nature, and our values. The TRC Committee, Senator Murray Sinclair, Chief Willy Littlechild, and Dr Marie Wilson, did a tremendous job for our people. I am also very proud to say I am directly related to Senator Sinclair; his mother, Florence, and my father, Elijah (both now deceased), were cousins, and come from Fisher River Cree Nation.

I believe that the TRC has developed and made a "road map" and set us off to reconciliation. It's up to both sides to make it happen, to find that peace, happiness, and contentment of living and sharing our country together as one united family. The historical research coupled with Survivor testimony has made a complete document about the experiences of Indigenous students who attended these schools. I know other Survivors of the same system have not been recognized but for now, the Final Report is the best that we have.

I believe that Canada will change, but I also believe that had it not been for the will and the tenacity of all Survivors of the colonial system to hold on to our culture, our heritage, and our way of life, Canada may have never have come forward to do the right thing for residential school Survivors. Now they must apologize and provide justice to all Survivors across Canada.

There are thousands of Survivors who were distanced from their parents, their community, and their culture emotionally, even if not physically like the residential school Survivors. These people were not included in the compensation package because the institutions they were put in were not classified as a residential school, like Teulon, Manitoba. There are approximately 478 schools across the country on what Canada calls the "Unvalidated Indian Residential Schools' List."[4]

The TRC's call to action #46 calls for "Enabling those excluded from the Settlement Agreement to sign onto the Covenant of Reconciliation," and we hope that Canada will respect this concern, because day school Survivors still need justice and financial compensation in the same manner as the IRSS Survivors.[5] They deserve the same kind of consideration with a similar package deal that was made with the Indian Residential School Survivors.[6]

Although most of the truths have been brought forward, there are still many aftereffects that will haunt our people for a very long time to come. We all know that healing does not happen overnight. As you may or may not know, there was trauma that our soldiers suffered while being in a war that was similar to what the Survivors suffered as well. However, seeing other Survivors get what they deserve is extremely gratifying and kept me moving on the tough days.[7]

I have found another Call to Action especially pressing in our current time as people quickly judge Indigenous ways of life because they have never been educated on what occurred. In 2003, during our first strategic presentation, Spirit Wind and I stated, "Education and communication with the public to publicize the individual and collective experiences of Survivors to the public are priorities of Spirit Wind. The Churches, public schools and universities have been identified as avenues for promoting the history of Residential Schools and to ensure that the stories of Survivors are passed from generation to generation of First Nations people."[8]

This aligns with Call to Action #62 which states, "We call upon the federal, provincial, and territorial governments, in consultation and collaboration with Survivors, Aboriginal peoples, and educators, to: Make age-appropriate curriculum on Residential Schools, Treaties, and Aboriginal peoples' historical and contemporary contributions to Canada a mandatory education requirement for Kindergarten to Grade Twelve students."[9] This is further explained in Call to Action #63: "We call upon the Council of Ministers of Education, Canada to maintain an annual commitment to Aboriginal education issues, including: Developing and implementing Kindergarten to Grade Twelve curriculum and learning resources on Aboriginal peoples in Canadian history, and the history and legacy of Residential Schools."[10]

The full contemporary history and legacy of these institutions needs to be explained by Survivors and this book has attempted to fill in some of the missing pieces. We believe educating people about the crimes that were committed is the best chance that this form of cultural genocide will never happen again.

Canada must know that a vast number of students did not return from these schools. Some of them died trying to get home, by following the railroad tracks in very flimsy clothing and poor footwear. Many died of the physical abuses that they endured at the cruel hands of the staff at these Indian residential schools. Some may have starved to death. Some young women became pregnant by male staff members and killed themselves because of this. Some babies were taken, given away, kept secret. We were too young, too innocent to know all the disgusting details of these horror events that took place. Only those bones left at these institutions can assure you about what happened there.

However, like the soldiers that came from the wars, it is much too traumatizing to relive it once again. So, therefore, our lips are sealed and our experiences locked away somewhere. We have already lived our hell, at the church-run Indian residential schools. May God forgive them for the holocaust. We did not deserve this treatment whatsoever. Until Canada addresses the issues as stated in the TRC Final Report, reconciliation will not be 100 percent possible.

9 CONCLUDING THOUGHTS: DIGGING UP BONES

As I reflect on where I am now, I guess I can say that I am well on my way to "reconciliation" and healing in my own way by praying daily to my Lord and Saviour, the Creator. Each day, I pray in the morning and at night before I go to sleep. I ask for forgiveness, guidance, love, and understanding of my fellowman. My recovery has not been easy, but the more I speak out and tell other people about my experiences, the stronger I seem to get. We all know why I am writing this legacy of mine. I hope that the people at large will learn about us, the "original five people" who were in the trenches in the early days, and who did so much for our people, the grassroots Survivors.

Let me tell you that it was not easy writing this book, it was like "digging up bones." It brought back many memories, memories that I would like to leave behind and buried forever. But I had to do it, despite the times I had to sit back, weep, and pick myself up so that I could carry on writing and telling my story.

It also hurts to think of the Survivors, including the "original five" Spirit Wind committee members, who sacrificed so much without any compensation, especially for those who have passed on without any acknowledgments for their efforts.

Despite all of this, I feel okay with what has been written in this book and I hope it will give some insight on all the people who also made the IRSSA. Writing this book has also given me the strength to carry on with the work that still needs to be done for the Indian day school Survivors. Reconciliation is so hard to accomplish as everyone has their own interpretation of what reconciliation is, but we must try to live in harmony and share our resources equally so we can be self-determinant.[1] I believe reconciliation will never happen one hundred percent in Canada because, as long as you have Survivors who have not been treated equally or have passed away before they were able to reconcile, it will be physically impossible.[2] The people of Canada must understand and learn that we were the original landholders and any compensation that is provided to Survivors is a way of "paying rent."[3]

Today, I also travel on a few occasions to schools and universities for speaking engagements with my son, Kyle J. Mason; we talk about our personal experiences, and how the Indian residential school system has affected our relationships as "father–son." In October 2016, we were invited to Providence University College in Steinbach, Manitoba.

We spoke to young students who were amazed what we both had been through, how we forgave each other, and how we learned to understand each other, to respect and to love each other in spite of what we went through. It has been very difficult to realize how my experiences in residential school affected my family. It was very painful, but it is ultimately a healing process for me and for my family.

Today, I watch my son, Kyle, perform his duties as an ordained minister and founder of the North End Family Centre in North Winnipeg. Through the Family Centre, his staff and him help people get back on their feet and be productive citizens of Winnipeg. His centre provides a meeting place, coffee, computer resources, resume writing, research and placements services, and laundry facilities. He makes his clients feel at home and throws birthday parties, Christmas parties, and other social events for the people who depend on this family centre. Since opening the facility in 2008, the group has raised over 3 million dollars in private donations and serves over 1400 community members monthly. In 2013, he was awarded the Queen Elizabeth II Diamond Jubilee Medal for his leadership efforts and making such a big difference in Winnipeg. I am so proud of my son's accomplishments and how he has handled the intergenerational effects of residential schools. His spirit has continued to be a source of my inspiration in forgiveness and helping all Survivors' children receive the support they deserve.

Over the last three decades in particular, I have been able to see the direct progress many Indigenous people and communities are achieving after our painful truths about schooling under the colonial system have been revealed. However, our communities are still dealing with high levels of drug addiction, incarceration, and suicide and low educational attainment levels as our generations cope with the legacy of residential schools and day schools. Spirit Wind realized in 2003 "the legacy of the Indian

Residential School System is intergenerational and it can be argued, the root cause of much of the social dysfunction experienced by First Nations people and communities."[4] However, healing takes time and we must realize that the intergenerational effects of the colonial system will continue to plague our peoples long after the Survivors have passed away. We hope that this book can inspire other relatives of Survivors to continue to seek justice in the face of adversity and keep progress moving forward.

In recent months, I have also been asked to attend two events on separate sides of the country that reinforced my belief that reconciliation is slowly, but surely, occurring. In July 2018, I presented a lecture and talk about my life at Queen's University, entitled "A Healing Journey and Walk towards Achieving Justice for all Survivors of Canada Who Were Impacted by the Colonial System." This was an emotional presentation for both myself and the audience as I talked mainly about the details in this book. I was blown away by the receptive students and welcome that the university showed to me and to my wife.

Despite the university being located off Sir John A. Macdonald Boulevard and in the middle of this prime minister's former city of residence, universities are beginning to separate themselves from this historical baggage in order to grasp a fuller understanding of what occurred under the colonial policies first enacted under the banner of Canada by our first prime minister. There has now been nearly three decades of research, learning, and discovery about Indigenous peoples in this country, but we must implement these evidenced-based solutions for our current issues. My talk lasted for over an hour and the audience provided engaging questions that let me know they were interested in achieving true reconciliation. The program I was presenting to was the World Indigenous Studies in Education (WISE) graduate program, which was founded in the early 1990s and has continued to offer a Masters in Education focusing on Indigenous ways of understanding the world. Times are slowly but surely changing to value both perspectives in education but also numerous other fields. It is remarkable that in my lifetime we went from trying to remove our spirit to helping foster and embrace our understandings.

That same month, I was also invited to present at the Thirty-Ninth Assembly of First Nations annual meeting in Vancouver to provide an update on the day school class action. The previous month our lawyers had been able to certify our case and we provided updates to everyone in

39th Annual General Assembly
Assembly Of First Nations

Raymond at Assembly of First Nations, 2018. Screenshot from AFN Annual General Assembly, used with permission of Jenna Young Castro, Communications Officer, Assembly of First Nations.

attendance. I said to the largest crowd I had ever addressed, "We're almost there you know. We have our foot in the door, but we still have a way to go, you know? A little ways to go still, and I'm sure with our legal counsel it will happen. We can all get what we deserve and that is justice, compensation, and respect."[5]

As our national class action continues to gather steam, I can finally see the finish line on the horizon; however, I won't stop fighting for our rights until I have passed away. This past April, I had a significant health scare which left me in the hospital a few weeks after doctors believed I was developing a brain tumour behind my eye. Before I went in for the six-hour biopsy, I went to the same Elder who had granted the name of Spirit Wind so many years ago. He told me that I should not be worried as the tumour was not cancer and I would be able to continue our mission. As the doctors came back with the results of the biopsy, I told them I already knew it was non-cancerous, but thanks for confirming with modern tools.

As this story hopefully demonstrated, our people have shown a resilient spirit in spite of the difficulties we have faced. The cover of this book is a reminder to our grassroots background and painted by the Indigenous artist Randy Sutherland Jr. When we ran away from the schools, many people told us to follow the railway tracks home as they all connected to various communities. We did not know that the police were always waiting on the tracks as it was the easiest way to catch someone who was missing as they intersected with roads and other towns.[6] Randy painted the big dipper as a symbol that always points north and to use the stars as guidance rather than the crossroads of railway tracks that led to the white authorities. The image shows an Elder telling a young person to follow these constellations if they are ever lost.[7] This image characterizes what Survivors have learned throughout the process of colonialization – to always follow our universe and ways of understanding the world.

I hope that one day I can also heal my relationships with a few of my mother's children. I hope that the gap in time between us has not become too great a problem to solve. I still think the world of them and love them very much. I hope that they can forgive what has happened in the past with myself and their mother, so that we can heal together. I know forgiveness is difficult and sometimes not warranted.

Today, I have now married my wife, Rhoda Mae Forster. What a wonderful experience this has been for me. I am so grateful for this second chance to learn what it means to have a family and to be a good husband and father.

In closing, it was quite a journey writing this book. I only hope that it gives readers more insight into the formation and development of the Indian Residential School Survivors Agreement. I hope they will see that it took many people to help bring it about and that they will appreciate all the volunteer work of the grassroots people, the Survivors of Spirit Wind. Writing this book has been a form of closure as my thoughts become realized and reinforced on paper.

AFTERWORD: TRUTH, RECONCILIATION, AND RESHAPING OF CANADA'S HISTORY

This is a profound commitment to establishing new relationships embedded in mutual recognition and respect that will forge a brighter future. The truth of our common experiences will help set our spirits free and pave the way to reconciliation.

TRUTH AND RECONCILIATION MANDATE, *Schedule N of the Indian Residential School Settlement Agreement*

"Ray, is it alright if we use the word 'story' to refer to what we are writing? Is there a word in Cree or Ojibwe, maybe, that we ought to use instead of 'story'? What do you say?"

"I don't like the word 'story.' Stories can be made up. This is the truth. It is my legacy. It isn't a story. These are my lived experiences. But I asked others and was told, 'Well, that's true, but it's all still a story.' So, you can use the word 'story.'"

The Story of How We Got Here

In January 2018, Kevin Lamoureux, the education lead for the National Truth and Reconciliation Centre hosted at the University of Manitoba, gave a lecture at Queen's University. It was entitled "The Role of Public Schools in Advancing the Calls to Action from the Truth and Reconciliation Report." This was the third of his public lectures that one of us had attended, as he toured various schools and universities in Ontario talking about reconciliation.

Lamoureux spoke about his own personal history and the essential role of schools in helping foster authentic reconciliation among Indigenous and non-Indigenous peoples through curriculum development. The lecture was held at Duncan McArthur Hall, home to Queen's University's Faculty of Education, which had invited Lamoureux to speak as part of the commemoration of its fiftieth anniversary.

Lamoureux expertly wove his personal history with Canada's history and the treatment of Indigenous peoples to demonstrate how everyone has a part in reconciliation and in paving a new path forward. He focused on two of the Truth and Reconciliation Commission of Canada's ninety-four Calls to Action, which he deemed the most important, particularly for budding educators.

62. i. Make age-appropriate curriculum on residential schools, treaties, and Aboriginal peoples' historical and contemporary contributions to Canada a mandatory education requirement for Kindergarten to Grade Twelve students

63. Call upon the Council of Ministers of Education, Canada to maintain an annual commitment to Aboriginal education issues.

   i.   Developing and implementing Kindergarten to Grade Twelve curriculum and learning resources on Aboriginal peoples in Canadian history, and the history and legacy of residential schools.

   ii. Sharing information and best practices on teaching curriculum related to residential schools and Aboriginal history.

   iii. Building student capacity for intercultural understanding, empathy, and mutual respect.

   iv. Identifying teacher-training needs relating to the above.[1]

Education, Lamoureux explained, was the reason that Indigenous students were forced from their homes in the past, but it now must be the source of preserving their culture and keeping their histories intact. The TRC's Calls to Action mention the word "history" twenty-six times on eleven pages of recommendations. Specifically, the phrase "the legacy and history of the Residential Schools" appears numerous times, insisting that this history must be taught to Canadians if they are to understand the impact these schools had on Indigenous communities.[2]

We thought about the reason that we had both chosen to study at the Faculty of Education at Queen's University in the first place (albeit, nearly twenty-five years apart). The faculty was entering its fiftieth year and its history was intimately tied to the origins of the Living and Learning Report (also known in Ontario as the Hall-Dennis Report), which was published in the same year as the faculty was formed (1968) and which had recommended some radical revisions to Ontario's education system. The opening sentence reads, "The underlying aim of education is to further man's [sic] unending search for truth. Once he [sic] possesses the means to truth, all else is within his grasp. Wisdom and understanding, sensitivity, compassion, and responsibility, as well as intellectual honesty and personal integrity, will be his guides in adolescence and his companions in maturity. This is the message that must find its way into the minds and hearts of all Ontario's children."[3]

The Faculty of Education at Queen's enshrined these beliefs in its philosophy as it began educating teachers in 1968. The basic principles included the "supreme obligation to foster the intellectual outlook and to pursue with steadfastness and humility the search for goodness, beauty and truth."[4] The first dean, Vernon Ready, who was a supporter of the report, stated, "The Faculty of Education's philosophy is based on the belief that knowledge, skills, and an expanding human spirit are the three requisites of a great teacher: We feel that what is learned in a school or college may often be derived less from formal instruction than from the experience of living and working in the institutional environment. In addition, we are convinced that there is not one single curricular programme which is equally suitable for all candidates; their backgrounds, their needs, and their aspirations are so varied that to prescribe an identical course of study for all seems highly questionable."[5]

In contrast to Ready's lofty words about educational ideals, much of our story has focused on some of the darkest crimes that Canadian schools have inflicted upon children. These children were innocent. They suffered because they were Indigenous.

We work and study in an institution that is explicitly taking steps towards realizing the TRC's Calls to Action. Yet this is an institution, like most schools in Canada, built on a foundation of Eurocentric ideologies and Western traditions that allowed Euro-Canadians to seek their understandings while leaving Indigenous people out. Lamoureux called upon federal agencies to fulfill their responsibility, reinforced by the United Nations Declaration on the Rights of Indigenous Peoples, which confirmed

"Aboriginal peoples' inalienable right to know the truth about what happened and why, with regard to human rights violations committed against them in the Residential Schools."[6] The truth about what happened was surely different for every student who attended residential schools in different parts of Canada. Some courageous Survivors pursued this truth and received an official apology from the government and compensation for the physical, sexual, and emotional abuses they experienced.

We are not singling out Queen's University as an exemplar, positive or otherwise. It is, inescapably and obviously, our point of reference, as each of us has pursued doctoral studies here. Queen's was established in 1841, at around the same time as the first experiments in the residential schools were beginning in Ontario. Its Latin motto, "sapientia et doctrina stabilitas" ("wisdom and knowledge shall be the stability of the times"), did not initially relate to Indigenous wisdom and knowledge. It ought to, in the present and future tenses.

In his lecture, Lamoureux vividly related stories of residential school Survivors and spoke of how his work took him across the world, retelling this chapter in Canada's history. He expressed optimism for true Reconciliation (with a capital R). He stayed afterwards to talk to a long line of captivated educators.

We continued to correspond with Lamoureux following this lecture. Here, we were introduced to Raymond Mason. Questions about the lawsuit regarding the day schools quickly merged with Mason's own story of surviving three residential schools and his advocacy work with Spirit Wind, which organized other Survivors in Manitoba to fight for the Indian Residential School Settlement Agreement (IRSSA). Mason told us that he had a manuscript about his life, but that it needed editing. He was unsure of the next steps required to forward the work to a publisher. Moreover, Mason was battling a tumour in his eye which was decreasing his ability to type or work on a computer and thus to apply to publishers who might be interested in his life's story. Subsequently, Mason shared a draft of his writing.

We read through the manuscript, equally shocked by the abuse and injustice and inspired by the resilience in Mason's life story. We searched online for the Birtle Residential School, the first institution Mason had attended, and found that it appeared in the final reports of the Truth and Reconciliation Commission at least fifty-three times. Stories from Birtle involved horrific examples of physical, sexual, and mental abuse, as well as examples of the resilience of students who kept running away or starting fires to burn down the structures that contained them. In 1935, a school inspector would start an investigation into the Birtle Residential School, after ten students ran away from the institution.[7] He concluded that the problem was caused by homesickness, although he added that "the spirit that pervades the school" could be another logical reason for students not wanting to attend.[8]

This spirit was wholly destructive. Mason would attend Birtle Residential School approximately fifteen years after the school inspector's report. His story reflects multiple stories of many children at Birtle and other residential schools across the country who had attempted to escape a system propagating cultural genocide. We agreed to collaborate on a book that would complete his manuscript. It was important to Mason and us that this story be told from the first-person perspective, but that it should also be contextualized historically.

Mason never experienced a spirit of schooling that fit Vernon Ready's idea of education. When he was growing up, educational institutions devalued his intellectual, spiritual, and cultural heritage. Conversing with Mason helped us to recognize the many privileges that we had been granted.

We are grateful to Raymond Mason: he has served as our teacher. We have learned about Canada's history and, in particular, the history of Indigenous education. We have also learned about history education in general, or the teaching, telling, and writing of history. In this book, we have Mason's story: a history, a legacy, a lived experience that runs counterclockwise to the history we learned in schools. We also present our own history writing: footnoted, formatted, copy edited. The stories are interwoven, with Mason's leading the way.

Relationships of Mutual Recognition and Respect

It is fitting that you encounter only our words here. Many readers may not reach this point in the text, and this is perfectly acceptable. This afterword, and the endnotes, are supplemental to Mason's story. We are making sense of our role in telling this story for ourselves and for those readers who have kept on reading. We are writing as members of a faculty of education who are seeking curriculum reform in line with, and guided by, the TRC's calls to action

To the extent that we can, we do this in line with the TRC call for a "profound commitment to establishing new relationships embedded in mutual recognition and respect that will forge a brighter future."⁹ From the first stages, we have thought of this work as a set of conversations. Indeed, this project was initially structured in the form of regular, weekly conversations with Raymond Mason, which were recorded, transcribed, and combined with our ongoing archival and historical research based on the emerging story manuscript.

Mason's story provided more context for the official Indian Residential School Settlement Agreement, which we were seeking to understand, research, and involve in our teaching. In our work with teacher candidates, we pose the question: why study the history of education? While sundry responses come to mind, the most obvious is relevant here: because history is a testament to change. Change is not inevitable and not necessarily progressive, but it occurs.

Change happens. It reveals that agency is possible. We can make a difference in the world around us. Mason's story clearly exemplifies this point. It documents the tremendous amount of activism and resilience that was required on the part of survivors to testify against their abusers.

This work acknowledges the disastrous outcomes for Indigenous peoples in Canada that have arisen from colonialism: academic, intellectual, geographical, historical, and other. The meaning of reconciliation in the Canadian context needs ongoing consideration. We began this work three years after the publication of the TRC's Calls to Action. At the time, Canadian media were rife with stories regarding the deaths of two Indigenous youth: Colten Boushie from Red Pheasant Nation, Saskatchewan and Tina Fontaine from Sagkeeng First Nation in Manitoba. In both cases, the people charged with their murders were acquitted. These verdicts, coming within months of each other, drew attention and swift reaction from across Canada. Many Indigenous activists and supporters felt that a grave injustice, based on inherent racism, had been committed.¹⁰ These cases were personal for Mason. His home is located in Manitoba and one of the crimes occurred close to his community.

They speak loudly and clearly to the need for curriculum reform.

In the province of Ontario, the current curricula in both social studies and history focus on historical thinking and inquiry. They involve scrutinizing evidence, examining historical perspectives, considering the causes and consequences of events, and deliberating on continuity and change over time. A memorandum sent in November 2017 from Ontario's Ministry of Education to all directors of education, secretary-treasurers, and supervisory officers of school authorities stated that funding would be provided to respond to the Truth and Reconciliation Commission's Calls to Action (in particular, calls 62 and 63). As of the time of writing, this funding has not been provided in social studies and history.

The methodological approach for Spirit of the Grassroots People centres around three principles developed in *Aboriginal Oral Traditions: Theory, Practice, Ethics.* This collection of essays, edited by Renée Hulan and Renate Eigenbrod and derived from a conference on Indigenous oral traditions, provides the framework and valuable lessons for this type of history. The three principles are, first, that the historians/researchers be "accepted by the community and by leaders of a community"; second, that "information must protect the intergrity of the people and the community being studied"; and third, that "in most cases the information must be available to the community to benefit their future development."[11] These principles contributed to the generation of a framework for our research. Yet as Hulan and Eigenbrod note, "There is no standard methodology in collecting and analyzing oral traditions."[12] As primarily settler Canadians from southern Ontario, we had little experience talking with First Nations people from Manitoba. Yet we both sought opportunities for "intercultural understanding, mutual respect, and empathy," which Kevin Lamoureux believes to be central to reconciliation. Reconciliation can only be achieved if historically accurate biographies detail one of the darkest chapters in Canadian history. Mason's story, including his willingness to forgive and to work with two (primarily) Euro-Canadians, demonstrates a serious commitment to reconciliation.

A richer historical interpretation of the evolution of Canada's schools is important for all educationists, not merely historians. As Sylvia Moore states, "If we change the stories we live by, quite possibly we change our lives."[13] Since stories are so essential to who we are, and to the foundation upon which all our education and knowledge systems are built, they need to be historically based.

We collectively also decided that notes should be added to various sections to provide context and references, annotating but not interrupting the story. The notes do not add truth to Mason's story; they contextualize it. But one of the aspects that distinguish history from story is that the assertions made are based on warrants. We are crossing borders here: storytelling, history, oral history, and reconciliatory work.

After working with Mason for a few months at a distance, we realized this project would not be possible unless we met in person to record his life and talk about the logistics for this project. The Faculty of Education at Queen's University invited Mason to travel to Kingston in July 2018 as a guest lecturer (see chapter 9). This provided the opportunity for us to meet in person and record his story. These conversations took place over the course of several days, during which we slowly went through his life and the contributions of Spirit Wind.

Oral Histories

Several scholars have made it a priority to work with Indigenous communities and to create authentic oral histories with First Nation communities. Peter Geller, a non-Indigenous educator and historian in northern Manitoba, wrote an article entitled "Many Stories, Many Voices: Aboriginal Oral History in Northern Manitoba." He emphasizes "the power of oral history to voice the experiences and the historical understanding of those who did not often have a place within the conventional, academically oriented written histories."[14] His study focuses on the educational practice of using oral history in northern Manitoba so that communities can heal, and demonstrates that this is an effective method of transmitting information to future generations.

Furthermore, these stories are not meant just for analyzing and historically recording, but to inform present debates about a range of educational as well as cultural issues. As Neal McLeod argues, "Cree narrative memory is more than simply an academic exercise in archiving information and sounds. Cree narrative memory is an ongoing attempt to find solutions to problems that we face today such as breakdown of families, loss of language and a general loss of respect for ourselves and others."[15] Mason hoped to record his life's story so that people in his community of Peguis First Nation, along with his family and friends, could experience his narrative recollections through their traditional method of telling stories. The tapes that have been digitally recorded will be stored with Mason's family so that they can listen to any section whenever they want or need to do so.

This form of narrative yields new insights into our current issues. The story Mason has told in the previous chapters of this book needs to be carefully preserved and experienced in order to properly understand his life and to reveal the links between his past and our present.

From Oral to Written

Our decision to transcribe Mason's story into a written language has been informed by scholars who have done similar cross-cultural research. They point out that print enables the speakers to reach a much wider audience and helps them to find closure. In 1999, some leading linguists and Indigenous authors wrote *Talking on the Page: Editing Aboriginal Oral Texts* as a result of efforts to bring oral histories into written text. Edited by Laura Murray and Keren Dichter Rice, the collection makes several recommendations about the incorporation of Indigenous oral histories into a historical text:

> If a speaker's words are recorded on tape or in writing and then published, the potential audience expands, and the layers of mediation between the words' sender and their receivers multiply from their original context. In many cases, the larger audience (or readership, really) does not know enough, or have a strong enough history of relation with the teller, to understand the story in the spirit it was told. But … even the most intimate storytelling situation does not ensure identical understandings of a story. Even a grandmother and a grandchild within the same household experience the same story differently, as Basil Johnston observes in his contribution to [*Talking on the Page*], and in fact, this ability to carry many meanings is a large part of the power of stories.[16]

Walter Ong and John Hartley explain how writing can promote closure with the past as well as provide a means of understanding complex phenomena.[17] They note, "Print encourages a sense of closure, a sense that what is found in a text has been finalized, has reached a state of completion

... Print, as has been seen, mechanically as well as psychologically locked words into space and thereby established a firmer sense of closure than writing ... Under the author's eyes the text lays out the beginning, the middle and the end, so that the writer is encouraged to think of his work as a self-contained, discrete unit, defined by closure."[18]

Mason felt that having his story told as text provided him with closure. Having it written down freed him from having to remember it, offering a form of finality on a difficult period in his life.[19]

It is impossible to reveal Raymond Mason's vocal inflections and rhythms, or the emotional undertones that were experienced during our taped sessions. Still, we hope that the reader will be able to grasp the spirit and character of Raymond Mason as he explains his life in this particular context. Here, Mason's truth is still intact. The words are his. When transcribing and working through the text, we exercised control only over punctuation, allowing us to slow down or speed up the story, but not to change it. Mason sped up and slowed down, as he needed to, to tell the story that he needed to tell, and in manipulating commas, semicolons, and periods, we sought to match his pace. While tempted to use quotes, capitalization, and underlining, we refrained from altering the text itself. The story was ours to translate from spoken words to text, not to transform.[20] Moreover, each reader will be able to draw different meanings from the story by relating it to other experiences of Indigenous life in Canada. We believe that not to present this story in an accessible form that broadens its reach would be a disservice to the already silenced voices of other Survivors. Murray and Rice state, "Words not made public cannot serve to combat misunderstandings and ignorance in the general population; nor can they inform and encourage Native people living away from their elders in cities or serve members of other Native groups who might welcome the stories and strategies of another culture by way of comparison."[21]

Spirit of the Grassroots People, further, responds to a challenge Georg Iggers raises for historians in his review of the discipline.[22] In *Historiography in the Twentieth Century: From Scientific Objectivity to the Postmodern Challenge*, Iggers concludes, "There was no comparative intercultural examination of historical thought ... [and] this comprehensive perception is still lacking. The problems we have mentioned that make it difficult to write global history also confront an intercultural, comparative study of historiography. Such a history is still a project for the future."[23] In this book, we model some aspects of combining the oral history of Indigenous cultures and the written history of Westernized cultures. We see this as a new way forward in history writing, particularly as it relates to Canada's history of education with respect to residential schools. This way requires that there be collaboration between historical actors and subjects and academics and researchers. It involves multiple sources and multiple ways of interpreting data. It requires an ongoing, reflective, and iterative consideration of how such historical work draws us closer to an understanding of reconciliation in a Canadian landscape, a landscape that has been altered by the findings of the TRC. This work acknowledges Mason's oral traditions. It does not supplant them. Rather, it nods to two traditions, one Indigenous and one Western in its roots. It seeks to be two-eyed. Both perspectives can be used in writing about the past in order to inform our present situation.

Decolonization

Raymond Mason has been aware of the demands for truth among his community and other Canadians since the late 1980s. He has worked steadfastly to seek and tell the truth as he sees it through his own life experiences. Mason has an insider's perspective on the schools themselves, on the many legal developments that have occurred in recent years, and on working to achieve justice. These factors help to explain the impact of his words and the information they bring to other Indigenous people. The Truth and Reconciliation Commission reports published in 2015 seamlessly blended oral testimony and written historical evidence – a method with which Mason agrees – to provide closure for many of the Survivors. However, Mason contends that the story of Spirit Wind has not been accurately told. He contests the accepted narrative with his own truth.

In light of Scott Morgensen's work regarding clearance of research work through university ethics boards, we argue that Indigenous methodologies act as a significant practice of decolonization. As Morgensen explains, "Indigenous methodologies envision the termination of colonial rule by fomenting the knowledges of sovereign and decolonizing peoples: that is, knowledges that subvert the ontology of a perpetually colonial society toward radical transformations of land, life, and governance." These methodologies inspire "activism and reclamation of Indigenous histories and homelands."[24] In academia, pursuing the goal of Indigenous knowledge creation can help transform normative colonial ideas. As we worked together, Mason was in full control over the recording of his life story and was provided with opportunities to withdraw from sharing his recollections at any time. Most of the content in ethics board applications focuses on quantitative research and does not apply to a self-selected Indigenous oral history where no set questions would be asked nor was recruitment of participants necessary.

The field of decolonization theory has particular reference to this project. Mason believes that despite the efforts of the TRC, Canada is still not fully aware of the impact of colonial power inflicted upon Indigenous groups. Moreover, he is disappointed that Indigenous activists, some of whom have already passed away, were not credited with resisting the government's attempts to silence their voices about residential schools.

Pamela Palmater, a leading Mi'kmaw activist and scholar, has taken an active role in the decolonization movement. She argues that both media and governments see colonization as a sad legacy when in fact, colonization is a present reality and not a historical artifact. It affects every Indigenous person in Canada. She stresses that we need to "empower ourselves, our families, communities and nations with critical information and analysis to help overcome those barriers."[25] Like Palmater, Glen Coulthard has written about the problems with understanding reconciliation as only a historical issue and not an ongoing work in progress. He argues against "narrowly situating the abuses of settler colonization firmly in the past. In these situations, reconciliation itself becomes temporally framed as the process of individually and collectively overcoming the harmful 'legacy' left in the wake of this past abuse."[26] We wish to highlight that Mason's story exemplifies grassroots activism by Indigenous communities and by residential school Survivors that overcame many barriers and effected tangible historical change.

The Next Chapters

As evidenced by the numerous endnotes, this work would not have been possible without the publication of the TRC's final reports, and we believe this book is the next chapter in explaining the process that started the commission's investigations into the residential schools.

The process of writing this history was guided by Mason's own truth. Moving forward, we must incorporate new narratives that use a spectrum of cultural histories in the hope of achieving culturally relevant and historically based education for future generations. The Indigenous concept of "Two-Eyed Seeing" can be beneficial in creating authentic pedagogy. This process, which is now informing environmental sciences and ecological studies, incorporates both worldviews in learning about different understandings of the world.[27]

Two-eyed seeing has a range of definitions, depending on the author, yet it implies that "people familiar with both knowledge systems can uniquely combine the two in various ways to meet a challenge or task at hand."[28] The legacy and history of residential and day schools demand that we understand how they occurred, where we can help repair the damage, and why we need to realize that reconciliation is very much a work in progress. It involves self-determination by Indigenous people and just treatment of them by others.

Mason's story provides further insight into the lead-up to the findings of the TRC and the IRSSA. Our involvement in this book was deeply influenced by the methods the TRC employed and the historical truths they sought. At first, Mason was not a strong supporter of history, or of its ability to inform and contextualize situations. His previous experience with history classes during his time in school and stint in university reinforced his belief that Canadian history was for the "winners" or Euro-Canadians, and that it tended to leave out Indigenous history.

Mason has read the TRC final reports, which were created by a mixture of oral testimony and additional context added by historians. He believes that these reports bring greater legitimacy to Survivors' stories, and he wanted to add his voice to those of others transcribed in the pages of history. In this way, we can fulfill one of the first principles that Cheryl Bartlett, Murdena Marshall, and Albert Marshall outlined in their article "Two-Eyed Seeing and Other Lessons Learned": "Acknowledge that we need each other and must engage in a co-learning journey."[29]

Further, they argue, "We believe that if participants do not or cannot acknowledge that they need each other and that they need to engage in meaningful co-learning, then an attempt to weave Indigenous Knowledge and mainstream knowledges and ways of knowing is destined to evolve into mere show, the only question being how long that might take."[30] In this work, we have acted from the belief that learning from each other through the writing process, and actively looking for ways to weave traditional written history with oral histories, would produce something larger than the sum of its respective parts. To help repair the connections in Canada that have been damaged by colonialism, we need to make accessible forms of history. Our participation in this project is that of allies. As Joe Kincheloe and Shirley Steinberg observe, "It is important for Indigenous peoples to have informed allies outside their local communities. Such allies can play an important role in helping Indigenous peoples deal with the cultural, psychological and environmental devastation of traditional colonialism and neocolonialism." Indigenous peoples and settlers can and ought to work together to help eradicate the effects of colonialism. In this process, history education can serve a vital role.[31]

Two important points for understanding the use of history as it educates the public about the TRC have also been realized through this writing process. The first involves a recognition that Canadian history has been, and will continue to be, a set of stories told within a particular context. But as the context changes, new evidence comes to light and new perspectives are included. Stories are contested even as they are being written. Time passes, and history, as it was told, is now told otherwise. The study of Canadian history must bring forth a historical way of thinking, understanding, and viewing the world that provides room for both Indigenous and non-Indigenous cultures to survive. As Christou has argued, "One way of thinking about this is to state that schools do change. Schools can change. Schools will change."[32]

Second, Christou observes that "our personal educational histories, the memories of our own experiences in classrooms and schools, cut deep; so much time spent during such important stages in our lives leaves its mark upon us."[33] These marks can alter our own personal histories – as demonstrated by Mason's story. Even now, he is still coming to terms with what happened during his schooling. However, he grasps the point of Christou's question: "beyond these personal histories, which are rooted in our memories and stories, what do we know about the history of schooling, or the history of educational ideas, in our communities?"[34] Mason was unaware of the various contexts and factors that led to his terrible schooling experience. Through the process of writing this book, he was able to acquire an understanding of the residential school era that extends farther than his own personal oral narrative. This does not negate his experience but rather strengthens his understanding of the past.

To initiate larger reforms in education, the past experiences of students need to be examined. This includes gathering oral testimony, providing historical sources, and contextualizing social action, such as that initiated by members of Spirit Wind, in order to fully understand why our perceptions about schooling in this country have altered.

In the 1960s, schools in many parts of Canada used the history textbook *Canada: The Struggle for Empire*, written by Luella Bruce Creighton. This book tells the story of Euro-Canadians' efforts in "settling" in Canada and the numerous difficulties they encountered in the "New World." The first chapter focuses on the "unknown continent." Creighton writes, "For a thousand years after the coming of Christ, the unknown continent lay almost untouched, offering infinite treasure, matchless possessions, to anyone that with skill and daring might come to take them ... Century after century, throughout the summers and the winters, through all the days, under grass and under snow, offering feast and famine to the few and undemanding Red Men, the unknown continent lay waiting for its masters."[35] This textbook reinforced the colonial and European stance that minimized the cultures of Indigenous people. Its first "questions and research" school activity had the effect of diminishing the contributions made by Indigenous people: "Before the arrival of the white men in North America, most of the inhabitants were living the kind of life that had been lived by men of the New Stone Age (Neolithic Age) in Europe and Western Asia. Find out: (a) when these other New Stone Age men lived; (b) why their age was called the New Stone Age. Compare their lives and achievements with those of the North American Indian."[36] This book was accepted and promoted in schools. The content was taught to Euro-Canadian children and Indigenous students, including Ray Mason, who attended residential schools and Indian day schools. It conveyed to all students the superiority of the settler (Western) ways of understanding the world, indicating that they had evolved more efficiently and accurately than those of Indigenous peoples.

The third question in the first school activity seems particularly relevant to the Cree peoples and especially to Mason's life experiences. Creighton prompts students as follows: "The Indians were still savages when the white men arrived, but the Agricultural Indians and the Pacific Coast Indians were perhaps closer to civilized life than the others. Suggest reasons for this."[37] Indigenous peoples were continually seen as "savages" who required residential schools to help civilize them.[38] Arguably, in the eyes of historians at the time, this process was easier for Indigenous societies who had similar societal structures to those of the Europeans and who were not nomadic.

Even into the late 1980s, colonialism was the historiographical lens used by some historians in their interpretation of the past. One of the essential secondary sources (in fact, the only official one) for the history of Thompson, Manitoba, is Graham Buckingham's *Thompson, A City and Its People*, which was published in 1988 by the Thompson Historical Society. Praised in the Manitoba legislature, this book was said to be "an excellent opportunity to reflect on Thompson's past and just how much has been accomplished in such a short period of time."[39] Thompson was by this time the third largest city in the province. Despite all the facts that the book provides to people interested in this community's development, the colonial shroud still surrounds it. For example, Buckingham notes, "By the beginning of 1962, Thompson was established. That is to say, the town was fulfilling its purpose, not only by providing a glimmer of the light of civilization in an otherwise dark and forgotten area of the world. The rudimentary needs of Western culture were now in place; houses, shops, hydro, sewage disposal, communication with the rest of the world (albeit limited), recreational facilities, churches, schools, service organizations and clubs were all operating and functioning well."[40] In this version, the civilized world of Western culture with all of the modern necessities would bring a light that was supposedly nonexistent to the Cree people who had lived and travelled throughout the area for hundreds of years before the Europeans arrived.

This singular perspective changes slightly, as Buckingham documents the presence of Indigenous people in Thompson in other sections of his historical account. For example, he explains the Indigenous contribution in creating the first camp in 1956; at that time there were "approximately one hundred fifty people living at Moak Lake including about eighty Indians who were employed to do the labouring jobs such as clearing the campsites, and constructing fire breaks."[41] The Indigenous people were thus essential in helping the first geologists and INCO employees solidify their findings and thereby pursue a multimillion-dollar economic investment.

Buckingham explains a photo of a stop sign in both Cree and English in the following footnote: "Talk about bilingualism! Thompson's mixed population requires a double expressing of regulations on the street signs. Here is one of the town language signs in the northern town."[42] Yet the Indigenous perspective is merely a footnote to a larger narrative about how the new town was constructed to "look ahead to a further growth and development in a community characterized throughout its history by a clear sense of vision."[43] Minor historical points are provided about Indigenous peoples but this book, written nearly thirty years after Creighton's textbook, represents negligible progress towards embedding an accurate Indigenous presence and perspective into our collective histories.

One of the history textbooks used in high school and university classrooms today stands in stark contrast to the books written by Creighton in 1960 and Buckingham in 1988. The fifth edition of *A History of the Canadian People* by J.M. Bumsted and Michael C. Bumsted, published in 2016, demonstrates the progress that is being made around knowledge of Indigenous worldviews, perspectives, and issues. In the first chapter, a set of questions is provided with the intention of solidifying students' learning. The first asks: "Give three examples of the ways in which the First Nations lived in a reciprocal relationship with nature."[44] This is a significant change from the 1960 textbook, as an attempt is being made to show that Indigenous worldviews are understood and valued. The third question shows how our historical understanding of First Nations has significantly changed from previous interpretations. It asks students to "explain the basic cultural, religious and political factors behind the European misinterpretation of First Nations."[45]

In roughly seventy years, or the lifetime of Raymond Mason, textbooks in Canada have undergone significant changes in regard to Indigenous histories. These interpretations had previously been absent from our understanding of the past, but today textbooks are beginning to offer alternative insights into Canadian history. Mason's story highlights how Indigenous people were actively involved in fighting for accurate representation through official investigations into the IRSSA. His voice, along with the spirit of the grassroots people, has contributed to correcting the historical mistakes that were once reinforced by school textbooks. A movement towards including Indigenous history in mainstream historical writing can be detected which, if continued, will influence our communal understanding of the past.

History should be a collection of oral testimony, written records, and a combination of the interpretations of previous historians who have attempted to tell these stories in the most effective manner for their individual circumstances. Christou highlights this view: "Historical study is most meaningful when exploring our worldviews and the meanings of what it means to be human. The fundamental purpose of historical study, akin to the aporia that was central to classical philosophy, must concern our wondering about how to live well and ethically. History is a means of engagement with who we are – individually, collectively, culturally, diversely – on this planet."[46] The societal contexts of the past – who people were – interacted with each other to produce the devastating residential school system, which still affects Mason's life every day.

Christou explains that the "history of education, seen here both as a discipline of study and as an approach to schooling, traces stories marking the inevitability of reform and change across cultures and contexts."[47] Mason's story is part of the story of the Indian Residential School Settlement Agreement, which has led to reforms, including the Truth and Reconciliation Commission of Canada, whose reports have created awareness about the residential schools themselves. On a wider scale, this awareness is currently being incorporated into our cultural context in Canada as we learn from revised history textbooks about what really has happened to Indigenous peoples in this country.

The role of schools is a constant force in young Canadians' lives. Mason had to experience residential schools long before anyone knew the meaning of those words. For too long, Canadian society turned its back on the relationship with Indigenous peoples, with catastrophic results. However, Mason's message of forgiveness and seeking the truth for both cultures which now reside in Canada will hopefully inspire the next generations of Indigenous peoples and settlers alike.

There are truths we can find. As Raymond's story shows, the truth was always there, but our own understandings have been in the way of knowing it. We need to revise the ways we think about and understand history in this country by focusing on the spirit of individual peoples and societies. This includes two-eyed seeing – using Indigenous and non-Indigenous methods both of which have been developed, refined, and are instrumental to us understanding our collective pasts. Acceptance of both worldviews is the only possible route to understanding the networks that have influenced and will continue to influence our individual and collect-ive lives.

Mason's story is unique and singular. There are an estimated 350,000 survivors of Canada's residential and day school systems. Not everyone can or will share their experiences. Others, like Mason, have told their stories. Each narrative is unique and singular. Each telling requires great courage, as it is the sharing of trauma and hurt. No one speaks for anyone else.

Alison Norman, speaking about the Indian day schools as they existed in the nineteenth century, notes, "Too often in Indigenous history, in-dividuals are left out of the story in favour of generalizations about the community ... [Indigenous] Communities were (and, indeed, are) compli-cated places where people had diverse ethnic and national backgrounds, religions, and political perspectives."[48] Generalizing across these narratives is dangerous and inadvisable.

We value Mason's story. It stands on its own alongside other stories. It stands on its own in a space full of untold stories and others that will be told in time.

After the publication of the TRC reports, new testimony was made available through the publication of edited volumes, biographies, and autobiographies. These stories rhyme, but none recount the same experi-ences. Each occupies part of the void, but none can do so entirely. *The Sur-vivors Speak* is one case in point. It outlines the experiences of survivors who testified to the TRC, layering testimony within a thematic structure. "In this volume, Survivors speak of their pain, loneliness, and suffering, and of their accomplishments. While this is a difficult story, it is also a story of courage and endurance. The first step in any process of national reconciliation requires us all to attend to these voices, which have been silenced for far too long. We encourage all Canadians to do so."[49]

Mason's story echoes the testimonies of others. Some of the similarities in terms of content are telling, including "separating siblings, abuse, stu-dent victimization of students, fear, loneliness and emotional neglect."[50] Other similarities concern geography: Gordon Keewatin, who is included in *The Survivors Speak*, attended both Portage la Prairie and Birtle Resi-dential School. Keewatin writes: "there were older boys there that used to, used to pick on the younger ones, and I was starting to get picked on. But I always ran to my brother, always looked for him, especially if somebody come and start poking me."[51] One story rhymes with another story, but we are not corroborating narratives or looking for common trauma. We high-light the similarity but accentuate the distinctness of all survivors' stories.

For instance, others note that they attended integrated public schools during the day and stayed in a boarding home at night around Dauphin, Manitoba. Martina Therese Fisher explains, "It wasn't a good experience. Cause this was my first time too, going to the white system with the white kids and we weren't treated very well there. We got called down quite a bit. They use to call us squaws and neechies, and dirty Indian, you know. They'd drive by in their cars and say awful things to us."[52] These words, recounted more than fifty years after the events transpired, speak to the lasting hurt that all survivors carry with them to this day. They are linked because they share an understanding of the residential schools system and its impacts. They all look into what A.C. Grayling calls "the darkest part of the dark," and shed light on this darkness.[53]

One aspect of the light that we find in many stories is resilience. Despite the purposeful harm inflicted on students in the residential schools, the survivors fought for a better future. They did not let the trauma limit or define them.

Basil Johnston documented his experiences in residential schools with the book *Indian School Days*. Johnston focuses solely on his experience at St Peter Claver Indian Residential School in Spanish, Ontario, which was operated by the Jesuits. Johnston was one of the first to describe all the logistical details of how the schools were run on a day-to-day basis.[54] Similar to Mason's meeting with former students at St Regis Hotel, Johnston met with his former classmates in 1973 for "reliving the days in Spanish by recalling not the dark and dismal, but the incidents that brought a little cheer and relief to a bleak existence."[55]

Johnston uses humour as a tool to help him relive his experiences. His book recounts the physical, emotional, and mental abuse inflicted on students. Corporal punishment "was given out every night at seven for those who broke any of the rules." Johnston remarks: "we were brought up by hand and boot."[56] But Johnston also recounts the ways that students developed to remain human despite the strict control of the Jesuits.[57]

Rita Joe, a Mik'maq poet and survivor of the Shubenacadie Indian Residential School in Nova Scotia, published her story in 1996. Joe uses poetry and her writing to recount aspects of her life after leaving the institution. While she does not offer overt descriptions of the abuse she experienced,

Joe admits, "It is true bad things happened while I was there. You can't help having a chip on your shoulder if you are told, military style, when to go to the bathroom, when to eat, when to do this and that, when to pray."[58] Rather, she tells the reader to "Remember: I found the good."[59] Joe's abuse and hurt continued outside of the residential school. She has used her creative work, her words, and her poetry to locate and to describe that goodness she found throughout. For her contributions in promoting Indigenous art and culture, Joe was awarded the Order of Canada, which can be seen as paradoxical.

After Prime Minister Stephen Harper issued an official apology for the residential schools in 2008, a wave of new memoirs on the subject appeared. These include autobiographies by Ted Fontaine and Bev Sellars and works co-written by Joseph August Merasty (with David Carpenter) and Edmund Metatawabin (with Alexandra Shimo). Mason's story adds to the sum of narratives, offering new insights, as each must because of the uniqueness of the individuals doing the narration.

For instance, Ted Fontaine published *Broken Circle: The Dark Legacy of Indian Residential Schools* in 2010. Like Mason, Fontaine grew up in Manitoba. In two separate residential schools, he suffered sexual and physical abuse. He remarks, "I entered residential school a loved and loving child but changed under the care of the black-robed strangers."[60] Fontaine's use of the phrase "broken circles" describes how families were torn apart and how children, forced from their parents and siblings, created families of their own among themselves. He reflects, "It would take me years to understand that trust goes hand in hand with understanding why a loved one does things. Sometimes broken trust never heals." Fontaine also recounts his experience of applying for claims through the Indian Residential Schools Settlement, noting, "I could go on for days with more detail, but I feel lighter now. The burdens in my mind and in my heart have been spoken aloud and their power over me broken."[61]

Bev Sellars's *They Called Me Number One* was published in 2013. She recounts how she fell ill with tuberculosis before turning five years old. Sellars was sent to St Joseph's Mission Indian Residential School in Williams Lake, British Columbia.[62] She shares aspects of her personal life including experiences of alcoholism, racism, and her own mental health struggles. Sellars chose to concentrate on leadership in her community. First, she served as a band administrator. Then she helped to organize an inquiry into the RCMP concerning abuse of Indigenous people along with fifteen other local communities.[63] After being elected chief of Soda Creek Band, Sellars organized the "First National Conference on Residential Schools in Vancouver in 1991."[64] Sellars is optimistic about her future and the future of others, arguing, "Residential school did not manage to beat the Indian out of me and my Aboriginal pride just keeps getting stronger. I look around and I see many more like me."[65]

Joseph Auguste Merasty and Edmund Metatawabin are the most recent survivors who have recounted their experience in residential schools. As is the case here, these survivors worked with other authors to tell their stories in a format that suited their intentions. Both Merasty's and Metatawabin's experiences reflect and amplify aspects of Mason's story. Merasty, for example, still has the physical scars of the abuse and struggled with alcoholism after leaving St Therese Residential School in Saskatchewan. It took him time to come to terms with his trauma, and the recounting of his story played a role in that process.[66]

Metatawabin also spent significant amounts of time in his life fighting the court system for recognition of his abuse at St Anne's Residential School. His quest for justice began in the late 1980s and progressed into a court case during the 1990s, a timeframe overlapping with parts of Mason's story. Metatawabin explains, "We were part of a wave of cases against the authorities – the churches and the federal government – that ran the schools. Once word was out, the number of cases and victims escalated. In 1995, Mik'maq activist Nora Bernard filed what would become the largest lawsuit in Canadian history, representing 79,000 survivors."[67] Nora Bernard would present her findings in the same 2005 House of Commons Standing Committee that Mason and other survivors attended before the government finalized the details of the IRSSA.[68] She noted, "the greatest concern at this time is that the elders are being re-victimized, re-traumatized over and over again, and at the end there's still no closure and most of all no type of justice. The survivors who went through the ADR process were not justly treated."[69]

Metatawabin recounts the following with respect to his own court battle: "I have to believe it was worth it: the court cases have become part of a growing awareness that has shifted the public's understanding of native history ... These successes have helped us externalize the shame, slowly shifting our anger from the self to the wider system, easing the burden of rage and memory."[70]

Rita Joe, Basil Johnston, and Joseph Auguste Merasty shared stories describing how they and others channelled their collective anger into positive change in Canada. These stories must be heard. Sadly, Joe, Johnston, and Merasty have all passed away since publishing their stories. We depend on the courage of the storyteller as well as on publishers and allies to help make these stories available. Raymond continues to fight on behalf of other voices, as evidenced by his continual efforts to expand the umbrella network of survivors of colonial schooling attempts.[71]

The Danish philosopher Søren Kierkegaard wrote about the experience of education and how it continues to influence a person on a spiritual level after its completion: "What is education? I should suppose that education was the curriculum one had to run through in order to catch up with oneself, and he who will not pass through this curriculum is helped very little by the fact that he was born in the most enlightened age."[72] Due to the nature of his educational experiences, it would take Mason many decades before he could "catch up with himself" and see what really occurred in those residential schools. His age was never particularly enlightened, although colonizers saw themselves as bringing the European Enlightenment to a dark continent.

The study of spirituality is traditionally not accepted within scientific (enlightened) or mainstream educational endeavours. In fact, Cheryl Bartlett, Murdena Marshall, and Albert Marshall argue that "we need to acknowledge that today's mainstream knowledges and educational approaches are products of decades of diligent efforts to scrub spirituality and religion out of ways of knowing and out of curricula."[73] Elder Albert Marshall states, "This is what we truly believe. This is what reinforces our spirituality: that no one being is greater than the next, that we are part and parcel of the whole, we are equal, and that each one of us has a responsibility to the balance of the system ... Knowledge is spirit and it is the duty of Elders to pass that knowledge to the next generation in order for them to learn the knowledge that is held within them."[74] As Cheryle Partridge has noted, "our ancestors knew the importance of our interrelationships as brothers and sisters to everything animate and inanimate and their accompanying spirits."[75]

Mason recognized this "accompanying spirit" and he ran away, fought back, and eventually contributed to the effort to earn compensation for over 80,000 Indigenous people who experienced the same types of neglect. This spirit, which persevered through some of the darkest days of Canadian history, has continued to be Indigenous people's inspiration; further, it will determine how First Nations should be perceived.[76] Dennis Troniak was the first lawyer who heard Mason's case, and when he defended the group of Spirit Wind Survivors at Parliament Hill, he also described this inherent spirit: "one of the greatest stories of courage, of the strength of spiritual light over darkness, and of the victory of the human spirit over adversity is told in the lives of the Survivors."[77]

Jackson Pind and Theodore Michael Christou, 2020

APPENDICES

APPENDIX A

Apology from the Anglican Church of Canada

Anglican Church of Canada

May 26, 2017

Dear Mr. Mason,

I am writing to you to apologize for the part our church played in the Residential School system, and especially for what happened you at Dauphin Indian Residential School. What should have been for you a time of learning, growth, and love in your family and community became instead a time of fear, pain, and abuse. Our church has long since realized that our participation in this work was wrongheaded, that we played a part in creating a legacy of trauma.

We also have learned about the strength of Survivors and the reality of healing in the lives of those affected by the trauma of the schools. I pray that your strength and the support of your family and community will allow you to be on a journey of healing and hope. I know that will be hard work for you and for those who support you.

Though you participated in the IAP process some time ago, we have only recently received notice of your claim and of the experience it reflects. So, this apology has been delayed. I hope that it speaks to you, however late it maybe, of the real regret and repentance of our church

It is unimaginable to me that we were so careless with the lives of children, so disrespectful of the languages, cultures, communities and families that formed you, and so unaware of the consequences of that carelessness and disrespect. The courageous witness of thousands of Survivors and their families has helped us to understand and to look for ways to contribute to a better future. Thank you for your part in that.

I am grateful that you are taking the time to read this letter. It represents the sincere and deep remorse of a church that has participated in causing great harm, and as an apology to you, who suffered that harm.

Sincerely,

Archdeacon Michael Thompson, General Secretary
The Anglican Church of Canada, 80 Hayden Street, Toronto ON M4Y 3O2

APPENDIX B

Independent Assessment Process: Report of Decision-Maker, E-S442-10aM-00487, Claimant Raymond Mason, 18 July 2008. Pages: 16–21

Assessment of Adjudicator Anne Wallace, Q.C.

Overall I found the claimant to be a forthright and credible witness who spoke frankly and candidly to the best of his ability. When testifying about the abuse itself, Ray was forth right and did not speculate when he could not remember. While he was unable to clearly identify some of the perpetrators, I am satisfied that the incidents did take place. These incidents occurred when he was a student under the age of 21 at the school.

I found on a balance of probabilities that many key events referred to in Ray's testimony did occur as he has described them. I have outlined. The evidence in some detail here, but if I find it necessary to refer to additional evidence in my discussion of the compensation to which Ray is entitled, I will do so under specific headings.

b. Acts proven

Based on that evidence, I make the following findings:

- At Birtle school, the claimant was fondled, and digitally penetrated by the short, fat supervisor, in the shower and in the dormitory. This is sexual abuse at level three.

- A male supervisor had oral sex with the claimant. This is sexual abuse at level three.

- A male supervisor had anal intercourse with the claimant. The precise number of times this occurred is unclear, so I am not in a position to find that the anal intercourse was repeated and persistent. This is sexual abuse at level four.

- The supervisor, ***, fondled the claimant's genitals. This is sexual abuse at level one.

- The claimant was subjected to anal intercourse by the student, *** and other boys about whose identity he is unclear. With respect to those incidents where the claimant is unclear as to the identity of the perpetrator, I am unable to make a finding because I do not have sufficient evidence on which to conclude that the abuse was predatory or exploitative or that an adult employee of the school knew or should have known about this abuse as is required by this process. With respect to the one incident where the claimant does clearly remember that the perpetrator was ***, this abuse was predatory and exploitative both because the perpetrator was significantly older than the claimant (four years) and because the assault was occasioned by threats. This is sexual abuse at level four.

- With respect to the allegation of anal intercourse with a student named *** or ***, I do not have sufficient evidence on which to conclude that the abuse was predatory or exploitative or that an adult employee of the school knew or should have known about abuse of this kind as is required by this process.

- With respect to the sexual assault by the female supervisor at Birtle, the evidence that claimant was able to give at the hearing was that the incident involved fondling and masturbation. This is sexual abuse at level two.

- With respect to the allegation of fondling by the student, ***, the evidence at the hearing establishing's fondling. I do not have sufficient evidence on which to conclude that an adult employee of the school knew or should have known but abuse of this kind as is required by this process. Therefore, this abuse is not compensable.

- With respect to the sexual assault by the female supervisor at Portage School, the evidence establishes vaginal intercourse and masturbation. This is sexual abuse at level four and level two respectively.

- With respect to the allegation of fondling by the female students in Dauphin this claim is not compensable because I do not have sufficient evidence on which to conclude that an adult employee of the school knew or should have known about abuse of this kind as is required by this process. Having said that, I do accept that an incident like this took place, even if the claimant is unable to identify those who assaulted him.

- The physical assaults committed by the principal were horrific and may well have grounded a claim at the PL level in this process. However, the model requires that for a finding at the PL level a medical assessment is required unless Canada waives the requirement for assessment. Canada has not waived the requirement in this case. Therefore, this abuse is not compensable.

The most serious abuses in this case are those involving anal and vaginal intercourse which is sexual abuse at level four. All other proven abuses which are compensable are subsumed; however, I will take those abuses into account in assessing the harms that claimant has suffered. Because of the number of perpetrators and the length of time over which the abuses occurred I assess the maximum **44 compensation points** available at sexual abuse level four.

c. Harms

Compensation in this process also considers the harm caused by that abuse. While the application claims harm level five, the claimant's counsel advised after the person of interest hearing that the claimant did not wish to undergo an assessment because of the further time that would be required to complete the process. The claimant has restricted his claim under this heading to harm level three.

I accept the claimant's evidence as to the harms he has suffered. The harms began with bedwetting at the Residential School, as well as the guilt, self-blame and humiliation the claimant already felt at that same time. The claimant also suffered anger, sexual dysfunction, difficulties with relationships (at work, with women and with his children), addiction to alcohol, retaliatory rage, depression and suicidal thoughts, including one actual suicide attempt. He suffered a significant lack of trust in others. It was clear at the hearing that he still feels humiliation over what was done to him.

I have no trouble accepting Ray's assertion that the sexual abuse as a boy was a factor in the many negative impacts he described. While there were some other contributing factors as well, the plausible link has been established.

While some of the harms established might be found at harm level four or five, the claimant has restricted his claim to level three. I am satisfied that the harms in this case are therefore most consistent with a finding of continued detrimental impact at level three. The range of points available for harm level three is from eleven to fifteen. The harms suffered by Ray have been serious and are best reflected at the high-end other range. I assess the maximum **15 compensation points**.

d. Aggravating Factors

An aggravating factor is a circumstance that makes the proven abuse even worse. This process lists certain aggravating factors that, if found, can increase the amount of compensation.

The aggravating factors present in this case (which I have found to have made the proven abuse worse) are:

- *Verbal abuse and racist acts:* The supervisor called the claimant a bastard.

- *Threats:* Both the supervisor and one of the students threatened the claimant not to say anything or he would not be allowed to ever go home.

- *Intimidation/inability to complain/oppression:* The claimant had no one to complain to. When he tried to complain, nothing was done. The supervisor used intimidation because when the complainant didn't cooperate, he was forced to wash the stairs.

- *Humiliation and degradation*: The sexual abuse was both humiliating and degrading.

- *The age of the victim*: The claimant was as young as twelve years old when the abuse occurred.

- *Abuse of a particularly vulnerable child*: After his mother died, the claimant was a particularly vulnerable child because he was an orphan and had no one to go to.

- *Failure to provide care or emotional support following abuse requiring such care*: No care was provided when the claimant did complain.

If aggravating factors are presented, I am entitled to increase the number of points allowed for the abuse and for consequential harm. Because the factors present here are so serious, I allow an increase of 14%. Based on the 59 points already assessed, this amounts to 8.26 which rounds up to an additional **nine compensation points**.

e. Loss of Opportunity

The claimant has asked for compensation at loss of opportunity level three, which is periodic inability to obtain or retain employment.

Especially in the early years, especially when he was battling alcohol, the claimant could find work, but he was unable to keep jobs because of his drinking. He testified to one instance where, because of his drinking, he was fired before he even started the job. He quit school at one time, because of his drinking. When he was in the air force, he ended up having to leave because his anger and retaliatory rage got him into difficulties. He lost jobs because of his drinking. For a time in Winnipeg, he lived on the street. The entire time he was in Edmonton, because of alcohol he only had one job. Since he came back from Edmonton and has been sober, the claimant has been more successful in his employment and business activities.

On a balance of probabilities, the evidence does establish periodic inability [to] obtain and retain employment as set out in loss of opportunity level three. This loss is plausibly linked to the compensable abuse, especially because of the alcohol addiction and the anger and retaliatory rage. I assess **14 compensation points**.

f. Future Care

The claimant has produced a future care plan aimed at addressing the impacts of the compensable abuse.

Ray has not had any professional counseling since he saw Tracy Cook in Edmonton. At the hearing, however, he said that he is finding that he is not as strong as he thought he was.

Ray has also been involved in traditional healing. Through Spirit Wind, Ray has access to elders who counsel him and advise him on spiritual things. The elders help Ray with his problems. Ray find the elders to be trustworthy and sincere and his able to confide about what happened in Residential School. This helps Ray to feel content because he has someone helping him with is personal situations. This sometimes includes the abuse in Residential School. Ray consults with an elder between one and five times a month. A return trip to the elder on the reserve is about 60 miles. Ray takes tobacco to the elder and sometimes he takes gifts of food.

The future care plan includes a seven-day healing program in Morley, Alberta. Ray would like to go to Alberta because he is too well known in Manitoba because of involvement in Spirit Wind and because of his boxing career (he was once a Canadian middleweight champion). He travels explaining the Residential School resolution process to others. He wants to be somewhere where he can be a regular person and not be known. The program itself is an intensive healing program including individual counseling with a medicine man and sweat lodges. It involves purifying and personal cleansing.

The future plan also includes all-day monthly sweats at Peguis. Right now, Ray does not go to these sweats because he has been seeing the other elder. He has asked the elder who runs the sweats if he will advise him because it is somewhat closer. The elder has agreed. Ray wants to do this. Ray believes this will help him to gain the strength psychologically and mentally that he needs. "I still have a lot of crap I have to get rid of." This elder dictates the course of the healing process. Ray expects to find peace of mind if he pursues this healing. Ray had hoped that the hearing would "be the end of it," but he knows that he still has some healing to do. He wants to "shut the door on this legacy."

This plan includes the following:

Morley AB Healing Gathering

Mileage – Peguis to Morley 3340km x. 455	1519.70
Meals for Travel days $58.10 x 2	116.20
Accommodations 7 days @ $125	875.00
Healer Gifts, ceremony, honorarium	500.00
Meals for days at ceremony 7 x 58.10	406.70
Incidentals for 7 days @ $17.30	121.10
Subtotal:	$3,538.20

All Day Sweats at Peguis (two years)

Sweat preparation costs ($100 x 24)	2400.00
Healer gifts/Feast ($125 x 24)	3000.00
Meals for 24 Sweats @ $58.10	1394.40

Subtotal:	$6,794.40

Total Treatment Plan Cost:	$10,332.60

The steps taken by the claimant and the claimant's testimony at the hearing establish that he is committed to ongoing treatment to address the consequences of the proven Residential School abuse. The evidence also establishes the need. I find that Ray has met the criteria under this process for an award for future care costs and I find the proposed costs to be reasonable. I award $10,000 for future care.

D. Calculation of Points

Compensation Category	Level of Compensation	Points	Dollar Award
1. Acts Proven	Sexual Abuse level four	44	
2. Harms	Harm level three	15	
3. Aggravating Factors	Points for acts + harms =59 x 14%= 8.26 points [rounds up to 9]	9	
4. Loss of Opportunity	Opportunity loss level three	14	
Sub-total:		82	$129,000
5. Future Care			10,000
Total Including Future Care			$139,000

I wish to thank all participants in the hearing, especially Ray, for their participation in this case.

Signed at Saskatoon, Saskatchewan, on December 16, 2009.

Anne M. Wallace, Q.C.
Decision-Maker, Independent Assessment Process

APPENDIX C

Assembly of Manitoba Chiefs Resolution in Support of Spirit Wind, 15 January 2003

ASSEMBLY OF MANITOBA CHIEFS
GENERAL ASSEMBLY
LONG PLAIN FIRST NATION
JANUARY 14, 15 & 16, 2003

CERTIFIED RESOLUTION

JAN-03.15

Moved by:
Chief Frank Whitehead
Opaskwayak Cree Nation

RE: SUPPORT OF THE SPIRIT WIND FORMER RESIDENTIAL SCHOOL CLAIMANTS ASSOCIATION

Seconded by:
Chief Felix Antoine
Roseau River
Anishinaabe First Nation

MOTION CARRIED
Abstention: I

WHEREAS, the First Nation Residential School Survivors have established a grassroots association called "Spirit Wind"; and

WHEREAS, the "Spirit Wind" association will represent the voices of Manitoba Residential School Claimants and their families.

THEREFORE BE IT RESOLVED, the Assembly of Manitoba Chiefs will support and advocate politically on behalf of the "Spirit Wind Association" by establishing a working relationship that will assist in addressing the issues and concerns regarding Residential School claims to be dealt with in an expedient and equitable manner.

CERTIFIED COPY of a Resolution Adopted on January 14, 15 & 16, 2003

LONG PLAIN FIRST NATION, Manitoba

Grand Chief Dennis White Bird

APPENDIX D

Spirit Wind Strategy/Plan Presented to Assembly of Manitoba Chiefs, May 2003

Background:

The Indian Residential School System was a deliberate policy of assimilation by the Government of Canada and a blatant attempt to destroy First Nation cultures and language in Canada. The pain and suffering of First Nations survivors of the residential schools operated by the Churches on behalf of the Government of Canada reached national prominence in 1991 when the experiences of those that suffered abuse at the schools first became public.

Aside from the language and cultural genocide, many of the First Nations children that attended the residential schools suffered physical and sexual abuse that has scarred many for life. The legacy of the Indian Residential School System is intergenerational and it can be argued the root cause of much of the social dysfunction experienced by First Nations people and communities. Resolution of the issue of providing fair, just and timely compensation for the abuse and cultural genocide suffered by those who attended the Canadian Indian Residential School System is one of the most pressing concerns of Canada's First Nations. This is important for the healing of survivors and First Nations communities. To date the Government of Canada has not allowed a fair and just resolution process to be developed that takes into account the concerns and wishes of Indian Residential school survivors and their families.

Frustrated with the inaction of the Government of Canada, and their strategy and tactics to control the process without fair and accepted input from residential school survivors and their legal counsel, Manitoba survivors created Spirit Wind in January 2003. Spirit Wind is a grassroots non-affiliated association with the mandate to unite, represent and support Indian Residential School survivors in their fight to receive fair, just and timely compensation for the sexual, physical, emotional/psychological and cultural/language abuse they suffered. Political advocacy, education, public relations, communication and the facilitation and support of work being done by existing survivor organizations and groups are major goals of Spirit Wind. Spirit Wind was established to provide a direct voice for survivors and complement the work being done by legal counsel and First Nations organizations like the Assembly of First Nations and the Assembly of Manitoba Chiefs. Unity, resolve, commitment, strength of the spirit coupled with the development and execution of coordinated and well thought out action will be key to ensuring the success of Spirit Wind to help win just and fair treatment for all residential school survivors.

Since its creation in January 2003 Spirit Wind has been rapidly gaining key support as a grassroots voice for residential school survivors. A resolution establishing Spirit Wind has been endorsed by survivors across Manitoba and a strong resolution of support for the Association was passed by the Assembly of Manitoba Chiefs in January 2003. The Assembly of First Nations passed a strong resolution of national support for Spirit Wind and its mission at its national conference in Vancouver held from May 6–8, 2003. Individual First Nations and Tribal Councils from across Manitoba have also strongly endorsed Spirit Wind and have agreed to work closely with the Association to meet common objectives. Other provinces such as Saskatchewan, Ontario and Alberta have contacted Spirit Wind to establish similar grassroots associations. The goal is to have a network of residential school survivor associations across the country to pressure the government and advocate strongly to ensure fair and just treatment for all survivors across Canada.

Spirit Wind is a non-bureaucratic organization with direction provided by a volunteer Steering Committee comprised of First Nations survivors. The name Spirit Wind was provided by an Ojibway Elder and is being registered as a non-profit incorporated association.

Two successful general meetings of Spirit Wind have been held in Winnipeg on February 14, 2003 and The Pas on March 14, 2003. A successful meeting was held with Ontario First Nations and survivors in Eagle River Ontario with over 250 people attending including three Grand Chiefs and a number of other Chiefs. At the meeting strong support was given to the work of Spirit Wind and the development of a chapter for northwestern Ontario. Requests have also been received for meetings in Brandon, Thompson, and a follow-up meeting in Winnipeg. A "run" to Ottawa, comprised of First Nations youth running on behalf of residential school survivors is being planned to start June 2, 2003 starting in northern Manitoba proceeding to Winnipeg and ending at Parliament Hill in Ottawa. Media coverage is being arranged to ensure the message is conveyed to the public.

Spirit Wind Position on Residential School Issue

Spirit Wind strongly feels that it is imperative that the concerns of survivors are taken into account anytime any discussions or arrangements or deals are being made pertaining to residential school claims. No substantive agreements should be made until the input of survivors and their legal counsel is received to prevent the making of any decisions that may be to the detriment of survivors or their families. Many survivors were victimized and traumatized at a very early age by their experiences in the Residential School System and they should not be re-victimized by a process, system and government that is unsympathetic and unwilling to recognize the pain, suffering and losses they incurred.

On May 7, 2003, at a meeting in Winnipeg. Manitoba Spirit Wind officially presented and tabled its mission statement resolution with the Deputy Minister of Indian Residential School Secretariat of the Government of Canada. The resolution (attached) was also presented to lawyers representing the Catholic Church, the Government of Canada and claimants at a April 23, 2003 meeting held in Winnipeg to discuss the tentative deal between the Catholic Oblates Order and the Claimants to provide compensation for those survivors who attended residential schools operated by the Oblates in Manitoba, Saskatchewan and northwestern Ontario. This resolution was the same resolution passed by the Assembly of First Nations in May 2003.

Key positions advocated by Spirit Wind on behalf of residential school survivors include:

1. Compensation must be considered and provided for emotional/psychological abuse, cultural and language genocide as well as the sexual and physical abuse currently being considered by the Government of Canada.

2. Everyone who attended a residential school should be entitled to some compensation for being taken away from their families and First Nations culture and way of life. The amounts should be provided individually with a minimum amount provided to everyone in consultation with legal counsel for the survivors.

3. The current proposals for the Alternative Dispute Resolution Process (ADR) must include compensation for all forms of abuse identified in point number 1 and not have any requirement (or waiver provision) that will limit or eliminate any legal rights of survivors for entering into this process.

4. The announced $1.7 billion total to settle the estimated potential 12,000 claims across Canada is totally inadequate. There should be no cap on total or individual amounts provided unless agreed to by survivors and their legal counsel as, in the opinion of Spirit Wind, no real potential value has been determined for the claims and this should not be arbitrarily set by the Government of Canada.

5. A maximum amount of options, including individual rights to legal action, class actions and out of court options such as the ADR process must be provided to survivors for their choice. This is why Spirit Wind passed and presented a resolution in support of the National Class Action in Ontario commonly known as the Baxter Class Action Suit in February 2003.

6. All claims are individual claims of survivors, and any money or compensation provided for their pain, suffering and losses is to be provided directly to claimants and their families. The Government of Canada should provide funding for First Nations cultural, social and languages as part of normal government funding as it does for French Canadians inside and outside of Quebec. Funding initiatives such as the support for First Nations languages announced by the Government of Canada in December 2002 must not be

considered as fair and just settlement of language and cultural abuse suffered by survivors and the funding for these programs must not be taken from money earmarked for the settlement of individual survivor claims. This was the approach taken in compensating Japanese Canadians and their families interned during World War II by the Mulroney Government in the mid 1980's even though the government was not legally obligated to provide compensation but did it because it was "moral and right thing to do according to then Prime Minister Brian Mulroney".

7. Second generation claims, filed on behalf of survivors by descendants must be recognized for compensation as the impacts of residential school abuses extend far beyond individuals to the families of survivors. This is especially true for those claimants who have, and unfortunately may die, before their claim is considered and settled. The Government of Canada and the Churches who operated the residential schools must not be allowed to avoid their responsibility for compensation by being allowed to delay and avoid the fair and just consideration of claims.

8. Coordinated and sustained political pressure must be placed on the Government of Canada to deal with survivor claims fairly, justly and expediently taking into account the concerns and wishes of survivors across Canada.

9. All administrative costs incurred by the Government of Canada, including legal fees and the administrative costs of the federal Indian Residential School bureaucracy, must be separate from the total funding of settlements. For example, the estimated $750 million administrative costs in the recently announced $1.7 billion ADR proposal, is totally unacceptable as it represents approximately 45% of all program costs. Reasonable compensation should also be provided to cover legal costs of the survivors.

10. The Government of Canada must ensure that all steps are taken to ensure that any process put in place to settle residential school claims does not re-victimize, humiliate or put undue stress on survivors and that the actions and tactics of the lawyers and others used to work on behalf of the Government of Canada and the Churches reflect this position.

Spirit Wind Strategy/Plan of Action

Spirit Wind, in support of the goals and objectives outlined in its founding resolution, its mission statement resolution (endorsed by the AFN) and the key positions stated in the above is developing a strategy and plan of action to start immediately. The intent is to develop a consistent and coherent strategy for all residential school survivors, complementing and supplementing the work currently being done by survivor's legal counsel, First Nations political organizations, individual First Nations and various residential school healing associations providing counseling and support to survivors. Spirit Wind recognizes that if these organizations and associations advocate "too loudly or strongly" they will be subjected to retaliation by the Government of Canada and may have important funding cut "often sold as saving taxpayer money or to improve the efficiency or effectiveness of government programming". Spirit Wind, being independent and not reliant on government funding will be able to put the concerns of survivors forward strongly and vocally without fear of retribution from the Government of Canada.

Spirit Wind's overall strategy and plan of action will be evolving, incorporating input from a variety of stakeholders and flexible to respond to changing events. Specific emphasis will be placed to counteract the divide and conquer tactics of the federal government. The goal is to pressure the Government of Canada to have the political will to consider and resolve the residential school claims quickly, fairly and justly.

Since 1993, it is clear that the Government of Canada's strategy has been to frustrate and control the legal process using unlimited taxpayer funds. The current Alternative Dispute Resolution Process (ADR), as mentioned earlier, is unsatisfactory and only deals with sexual and severe physical abuse, as these are the only categories of abuse that the Government of Canada will recognize to date. Spirit Wind has passed a resolution in support of the national class action lawsuit on behalf of survivors across Canada for compensation for sexual, physical, psychological/emotional, cultural and language abuse. In February 2003 Spirit Wind presented the resolution and spoke in support of the suit during the judicial certification hearing in Toronto.

As stated under its key positions, Spirit Wind strongly feels that all residential school survivors should have the maximum amount of options either inside or outside the courts for the fair and just resolution of their claims and not have to solely rely on a process that is arbitrarily controlled and dictated by the Government of Canada. It is important that the unfair position of the government and counter-position of Survivor groups are clearly articulated and communicated to the Government of Canada; the Churches; the national and international media; provincial governments; opposition political parties and individual politicians; the general public; and residential school survivors.

To carry out its goals and objectives the following have been identified by Spirit Wind as priorities:

1. Spirit Wind Coordination Support

Currently all activities of Spirit Wind are being done by a volunteer Steering Committee. With the scope and importance and urgency of the work that needs to be done full-time special events and fundraising coordination is required immediately. Spirit Wind has developed a proposal for the employment of a full-time fundraiser/special events coordinator (proposal is attached).

II. Communication Support

There is a pressing need to provide accurate, consistent and timely information on the myriad of developments, issues and concerns related to the settlement of Residential School Claims to survivors across the Province. This must include factual information through newsletters, regular information and meeting information spots through NCI and other media outlets, interviews with major media outlets, and support in setting up press conferences etc. Spirit Wind is also planning to tape meetings held and make available edited videotapes to First Nation communities across Manitoba. Estimated costs and budgets for communication will be determined in the near future.

Technical support and assistance in the development and circulation of Spirit Wind Communication material, developed by Spirit Wind, for circulation to First Nations throughout Manitoba and the media will be required. The proposed position of Fundraiser/Special Events Coordinator will take the lead in developing and distributing the newsletter working closely with AMC, MKO and the Southern Chiefs Organizations.

III. Meetings/Rallies

The February 14, 2003 and March 14, 2003 meetings in Winnipeg and The Pas were successful. Interest and requests have been received to hold similar meetings in centers across the Province as soon as possible (e.g. Thompson, Brandon, Portage la Prairie). Spirit Wind is also receiving requests to meet and talk with residential school survivors in smaller gatherings. These meetings will be coordinated with Spirit Wind legal counsel to ensure that accurate and up to date legal information is provided at these meetings. Funds will be required to cover Spirit Wind transportation, accommodation and meal expenses associated with these meetings. The parties requesting the meetings will be expected to make and cover expenses associated with the meetings (e.g. meeting room rental, lunches and refreshments). Rallies and protest marches in support of residential school survivors are being planned. This includes the "run" to Parliament Hill in Ottawa and highly publicized demonstrations. Individual First Nations will be expected to provide support for their people but additional organizational and support funds will be required. Fundraising, event coordination and detailed budget preparation will be done by the Spirit Wind Fundraiser/Special Events Coordinator subject to funds being found for the position. Spirit Wind will also require support to cover its costs and out-of-pocket expenses for its internal meetings and meetings with other First Nations survivor organizations and associations. These costs will be covered by the proceeds from fundraising events.

IV. Fundraising

To cover Spirit Wind expenses access to funds will be required to plan and carry out activities needed for the success of the Association. To maintain independence "no strings attached" donations will be relied upon. Spirit Wind has developed a proposal (attached) for a Fundraiser/Special Events Coordinator to develop and implement a fundraising campaign. It is hoped the position can be filled by July 1, 2003 or very soon after this date.

Bingos, raffles, and approaching all 62 First Nations communities to each donate $500.00 have been suggested as possible fundraising activities to raise money.

v. Other Possible Initiatives

The possibility of pursuing a separate class action suit on behalf of Manitoba Indian Residential School Survivors and taking the issue of the Government of Canada's treatment of survivors and their compensation claims to the World Court at The Hague were raised at the meeting in The Pas on March 14, 2003. Spirit Wind will be exploring the possibility of pursuing these initiatives.

Education and communication with the public to publicize the individual and collective experiences of survivors to the public are priorities of Spirit Wind. The Churches, public schools and universities have been identified as avenues for promoting the history of residential schools and to ensure that the stories of survivors are passed from generation to generation of First Nations people. Spirit Wind has co-sponsored a proposal to the federal Healing Fund Initiative to record and publicize the experiences of individual residential school survivors across Canada. It is hoped that members of the Spirit Wind Steering Committee will be able to meet with and make presentations to interested parties. This will be coordinated with a media campaign to ensure that the media, including mainstream and aboriginal newspapers, are informed on the issues and concerns with how the residential school issue is being handled from the perspective of the survivors. Assistance from the Assembly of Manitoba Chiefs and the Assembly of First Nations, especially through the Office of Vice-Chief Ken Young, will be required.

vi. Timelines

It is hoped that the Fundraiser/Special Events Coordinator can be in place by July 1, 2003 to work full-time on the above priorities under the direction of the Spirit Wind Steering Committee. A detailed plan and budget will be produced as soon as possible although due to timing some events may have to be started before a formal plan is developed.

vii. Next Steps

The Spirit Wind Steering Committee would like to meet no later than June 20, 2003 with the Grand Chiefs of Manitoba, AFN Vice-Chief Ken Young, and other individuals identified to discuss and finalize the following:

a. Agreement on the contents, and endorsement, of the Spirit Wind strategy/plan outlined in this paper.

    b. The working arrangement between Spirit Wind and the Assembly of Manitoba Chiefs, Assembly of First Nations, Tribal Councils and individual First Nations across Manitoba.

    c. Support and assistance that can be provided with no strings attached to Spirit Wind to carry out its work independently.

It is hoped that the meeting can be facilitated through the Grand Chiefs Office of the Assembly of Manitoba Chiefs and a resolution confirming this be passed at the May 2003 meeting of the Assembly of Manitoba Chiefs.

Spirit Wind Mission Statement

Whereas; Spirit Wind, is a grassroots network that unites into one voice and cause all Aninciabe Survivors who attended Indian Residential Schools throughout Manitoba and Canada.

Whereas; the Indian Residential School System operated by the Government of Canada and the Churches of Canada inflicted and implemented severe physical, sexual, emotional, psychological abuse, as well as a deliberate policy of cultural genocide, on generations of First Nations children across Manitoba and Canada.

Whereas; Spirit Wind is guided by the Spirit and provides Aninciabe People the strength, courage and conviction to fight for dignity, respect and fair, just and expedient consideration and compensation from the Government of Canada and Churches for our pain and suffering.

Whereas; Spirit Wind is determined to gain justice and healing for all Residential School Survivors and families that have endured ongoing pain and suffering as a legacy of the Residential School System.

Whereas; Spirit Wind is on a journey to educate the public, media and politicians on the destructive effects and legacy of abuse and cultural genocide inflicted on First Nations people throughout Canada.

Whereas; the Government of Canada must recognize that everyone who attended an Indian Residential School is entitled to and will receive fair and just individual compensation for emotional, psychological abuse and cultural and language genocide as well as physical and sexual abuse.

Be it Resolved; Spirit Wind will continue to grow across Canada and, unite, and advocate for, all residential school survivors until justice and fairness are achieved as guided by our Spirit.

Proposal for Fundraising and Special Events Coordination

<u>Submitting Organization</u>:   Spirit Wind Association (Association for Manitoba Indian Residential School Survivors)

Purpose:
To employ, and provide support for, a qualified individual to fundraise and co-ordinate special events to assist Spirit Wind in meeting its goals and objectives in support of the efforts of survivors of the Canadian Indian Residential School System to obtain fair, just and timely resolution of their residential school claims.

Background:
The issue of the pain and suffering endured by First Nations individuals who at-tended Canadian Indian Residential Schools operated by the Churches of Canada on behalf of the government of Canada reached national prominence in 1991 when the experiences of the abuse suffered in the schools became public.

Frustrated with the federal government's inaction to deal with compensation claims in a fair, just and timely manner led to the establishment of Spirit Wind in January 2003. Spirit Wind is a grassroots non-affiliated association created to represent and support survivors in the quest to receive fair, just and timely com-pensation for the sexual, physical, emotional/psychological and cultural abuse they suffered while attending Political advocacy, education, public relations, com-munication and the facilitation and support of work being done by other local survivor organizations and associations are part of the mandate of Spirit Wind. Spirit Wind will work closely with First Nations political organizations and sur-vivor legal counsel to provide a strong united voice for Indian residential school survivors. The Spirit Wind Resolution, endorsed by Indian Resolution School sur-vivors across Manitoba, which outlines the objectives and goals of the Association and the certified resolution of support from the Assembly of Manitoba Chiefs are attached for reference. At its May 2003 Annual meeting the Assembly of First Na-tions passed a national resolution strongly supporting Spirit Wind. Individual First Nations and Tribal Councils in Manitoba have also strongly endorsed Spirit Wind. A volunteer steering committee plans and coordinates Spirit Wind's activities.

Two highly successful general meetings of Spirit Wind were held in Winnipeg on February 14, 2003 and March 14, 2003 in The Pas, Manitoba where strong sup-port for Spirit Wind and its founding Resolution were received. Individuals from other provinces have contacted Spirit Wind to establish affiliated associations modelled on Spirit Wind. Spirit Wind has been contacted to hold additional large meetings in Brandon, Thompson and Winnipeg as the Association works to net-work with existing residential school groups throughout Manitoba and to meet and inform survivors across the province. A large-scale demonstration/march to publicize the issue and concerns of residential school survivors is one of many events that are being planned for the spring/summer of 2003. Plans are underway for a highly publicized march of survivors from across Manitoba to meet in Winnipeg and continue to Parliament Hill in Ottawa for a national demonstration of residential school survivors across Canada.

It is critical that adequate fundraising and planning are undertaken immediately to ensure the activities and work required are carried out successfully.

Proposal

Spirit Wind is requesting financial assistance and support for the hiring and employment of a fundraiser/special events coordinator for an initial period of twelve months to raise required funds and coordinate special events such as the demonstration march. The person hired will also play a key role in liaising with the 62 First Nations in Manitoba and facilitating two-way communication and information sharing with survivors across Manitoba. Efforts will be closely coordinated with the work being done on the residential school issue by the Assembly of Manitoba Chiefs, the Southern Chiefs Organization, MKO and the various tribal councils and First Nations across Manitoba. With Spirit Wind being non-affiliated and independent and not reliant on federal grants, the Government of Canada will not be able to put financial or political pressure on the Association or threaten to reduce or terminate other program funding for First Nations people.

Due to the pressing need to raise funds and start planning events it is critical that the position be filled as soon as possible. It is hoped that an individual will be in place and starting work no later than July 1, 2003. A brief position description that includes desired personal qualifications are attached for review.

An outline of the proposed maximum estimated 12 month expenses associated with this proposal is as follows:

Costs (July 1, 2003–July 1, 2004)

Fundraiser/events coordinator salary (plus 12.5% commission)	- $14,400 ($1,200 per month)
Office Space	- In-kind contribution
Telephone, fax, photocopier service	- In-kind contribution
Telephone costs (includes cell phone)	- $1,800 ($150 per month)
Office supplies	- $6,000 ($500 per month)
Personal expenses (gas, travel, meals etc. own vehicle provided)	- $12,000 ($1,000 per month)
Total	$ 34,200 (not including in-kind contributions)

Spirit Wind Fundraiser/Special Events Coordinator
Position Description

Position Summary:

The position will be responsible for fundraising and the planning and coordination of special events such as fundraising events, marches, protests, and general meetings on behalf of Spirit Wind. It will also play an important role in facilitating communication and cooperation with residential school survivors and the various First Nations Organizations across Manitoba. General and specific direction will be provided by the Spirit Wind Steering Committee. The position will report directly to the Chairperson of Spirit Wind or designate.

The position will involve frequent contact and liaison with various associations and organizations in the private, public and not-for-profit sectors. Close liaison and the development of close working relationships with the Assembly of Manitoba Chiefs, the Southern Chiefs Organization, MKO, Tribal Councils and First Nations in the coordination of special events will be required. The incumbent will be required to demonstrate initiative, develop needed ideas and activities, work with minimum supervision and be able to work with a variety of different individuals in a professional and diplomatic manner.

Experience and expertise in community fund-raising and the planning and coordination of special and or community events is essential. Sensitivity and experience in working with First Nations members, bands and organizations would be desired. Ability to speak one or more First Nations languages and interest and/or experience in the issue of Indian Residential Schools would be definite assets. Some travel throughout Manitoba will be expected.

Qualifications

Strong organizational, administrative, planning, coordination, entrepreneurial and interpersonal skills are essential for the position. Good written and verbal communication skills are required. Good budgeting, basic financial accounting and computer proficiency skills are also required. Ability to work independently with minimum supervision in sensitive and stressful situations is essential.

The position is a one-year term contract and may be extended or revised to meet the needs of Spirit Wind.

APPENDIX E

Assembly of First Nations Resolution in Support of Spirit Wind, May 2003

Assembly of First Nations
1 Nicholas Street,
1002 Ottawa, Ontario K1N 7B7
Telephone (613) 241-6789
http//www.afn.ca

Assemblée des Premieres Nations
1, rue Nicholas
1002 Ottawa, Ontario K1N 7B7
Telephone (613) 241 6789
http //www.afn.ca

CONFEDERACY OF NATIONS Resolution 1012003 May 6, 7 & 8, 2003, Vancouver, BC

SUBJECT: SUPPORT FOR SPIRIT WIND

MOVED BY: Vice-Chief Kenneth B. Young, MB

SECONDED BY: Chief Margaret Penasse-Mayer, Nipissing First Nation, ON

DECISION: Carried by consensus

WHEREAS Spirit Wind is a grassroots network that unites into one voice and cause all First Nation People who attended Indian Residential Schools throughout Manitoba and Canada; and

WHEREAS the Indian Residential School System operated by the Government of Canada and the Churches of Canada inflicted and implemented severe physical, sexual, emotional, psychological abuse and trauma, as well as a deliberate policy of cultural genocide, on generations of First Nations children across Manitoba and Canada; and

WHEREAS Spirit Wind is guided by the Spirit and provides First Nation People the strength, courage and conviction to fight for dignity, respect and fair, just and expedient consideration and compensation from the Government of Canada and Churches for our pain and suffering; and

WHEREAS Spirit Wind is determined to gain justice and healing for all Residential School Survivors and families that have endured ongoing pain and suffering as a legacy of the Residential School System; and

WHEREAS Spirit Wind is on a journey to educate the public, media and politicians on the destructive effects and legacy of abuse and cultural genocide inflicted on First Nation people throughout Canada; and

WHEREAS the Government of Canada must recognize that everyone who attended an Indian Residential School is entitled to and will receive fair and just individual compensation for emotional, psychological abuse and cultural and language genocide as well as physical and sexual abuse.

THEREFORE, BE IT RESOLVED Spirit Wind will continue to grow across Canada, and unite and advocate for all Residential School Survivors until justice and fairness are achieved as guided by ours spirit; and

FURTHER BE IT RESOLVED that the Assembly of First Nations provide political support for the establishment of Spirit Wind whose goals and objectives are to advocate, represent and advance the interests of the Survivors of Residential Schools.

Certified copy of a resolution adopted on the 7th day of May, 2003 in Vancouver, BC

Matthew Coon Come, National Chief

APPENDIX F

Raymond Mason's Presentation to House of Commons Standing Committee, 2005

Canada. Parliament. Standing Committee of Aboriginal Affairs and Northern Development. *Evidence*. 1st Sess, 38th Parliament, February 17, 2005. http://www.ourcommons.ca/DocumentViewer/en/38-1/AANO/meeting-19/ evidence

Mr. Raymond Mason (Chairperson, Spirit Wind Association):
Thank you, and good day.

My name is Raymond Mason, and I'm a Survivor of three different Residential Schools over a period of ten and a half years. I am chairperson of Spirit Wind, the grassroots Survivor association that was created in Manitoba in January of 2003.

At meetings held in Winnipeg and in northern Manitoba, Survivors endorsed the creation of Spirit Wind and our goals and objectives. Spirit Wind has also been endorsed by resolutions passed in 2003 by both the Assembly of First Nations and the Assembly of Manitoba Chiefs.

I'd like to say a few words about Spirit Wind. We are totally independent and do not receive any funding from Indian Residential Schools Resolution Canada or from the Government of Canada. Therefore, we are free to represent and provide a voice for Residential School Survivors without fear of having our funding cut as a form of retribution.

Unfortunately, oftentimes when important legal and political issues and large sums of money are involved, those who are the most important and affected but with little influence and power are often forgotten when deals and agreements are being made, purportedly in their best interests. Spirit Wind aims to prevent this from happening in the case of Residential School Survivors.

Spirit Wind intends to work with and not supplant the work of our elected leaders in organizations like the Assembly of First Nations and the Assembly of Manitoba Chiefs. Spirit Wind is supporting the efforts of the Indian Residential School Survivors Society in their work of organizing Residential School Survivors across Canada. We also support and encourage the work done by those helping Survivors deal with the pain and suffering they are enduring from their experiences at Residential Schools.

Spirit Wind's proposed purposes and objectives, supported by a resolution passed by the Assembly of First Nations and the Assembly of Manitoba Chiefs, are:

> To unite all Indian Residential School Survivors and their legal counsel to collectively facilitate: a strong ... voice for all Survivors; effective political and legal action for the just and expedient resolution of all Indian

Residential School claims; the educating of the public of Canada on the importance of the experiences and effects of the Indian Residential School System on First Nations people; and the publicizing of collective and personal experiences of Survivors through public relations and the media

That's quoted from the Spirit Wind founding resolution, endorsed by Residential School Survivors in meetings held in Winnipeg and northern Manitoba.

There are a few important principles that have guided Spirit Wind from its inception. First of all, financial compensation provided directly to each Survivor as part of the resolution process is fundamental for the government to address the Residential School tragedy. Survivors have strongly endorsed this position. They have told us they are the ones, along with their families, who endured the abuse, heartbreak, and impacts of Residential Schools. Healing is important but adequate and just financial compensation is the cornerstone of this. Funds provided for healing foundations and aboriginal culture are important, but they should be provided outside the individual settlement of claims. In short, these federal government initiatives should not be funded out of money that should be earmarked to pay compensation to Survivors.

For example, the Government of Canada spends hundreds of millions of dollars a year to preserve and promote the French language and culture in this country. Support for this established government policy is financed annually from government revenue. This principle should be extended to continue and expand aboriginal healing, language, and culture across Canada. Money for this should not come out of the pockets of the Survivors, many of whom are among the poorest and most vulnerable of our society.

Second, it must be remembered that each Survivor must be treated as an individual and afforded the dignity and respect of being able to deal with their pain and suffering and to pursue reconciliation and address as they see fit. They must be allowed the right to make their own decisions and not have others or organizations, even the ones that purport to represent their best interests, make deals or arbitrary decisions on their behalf. Each Survivor should be afforded the right to retain trusted and competent legal representation to resolve their claims. Those legal advisers must be involved in any negotiations about the future of the ADR or any other government redress program.

Third, the Government of Canada must acknowledge, recognize, and commit to fairly, justly, and equitably redressing the harm done. This includes providing direct financial compensation for sexual, physical, psychological, mental, cultural, language, and spiritual abuse. Any government program or policy to deal with the impacts of the Residential School tragedy must incorporate and include financial compensation for all these harms.

More than the discredited alternate dispute resolution system, better known as the ADR, a viable option must be available to Survivors to obtain redress. The ADR is being sold to Survivors and the public as a fair, comprehensive, non-adversarial, compassionate, and cost-effective out-of-court process to settle Residential School claims. Increasingly, the ADR process has fallen far short on all these counts, and I will say a few more words on this later in my presentation.

Spirit Wind strongly feels the class action approach for Residential School claims seems to be the only way the Government of Canada will listen and will take into account the concerns and suffering of Survivors. Therefore, in our view this is a preferred route to take. This, we feel, will ensure an efficient, timely, and court-supervised resolution process that will ensure fairness, equitable treatment, and consistency for all Survivors. It will also ensure that the federal government is kept honest and that it can not arbitrarily create or change the rules of the game, as they have been doing with the ADR.

Finally, each Survivor should have the opportunity to pursue their claims for compensation individually through the courts. They will be able to opt out of the class action process and pursue their claim individually if they wish to do so. In short, either way they will have their day in court. Regardless of which of the options is chosen by the Survivors, the horrors and devastation caused by the deliberate and systematic genocide against us must not be covered up and forgotten.

As you've heard and will hear today, the effects are widespread and intergenerational. The federal government must not only do the right thing but be seen to do the right thing in dealing with Residential School Survivors and the claims that are brought forward. To ensure this happens, their legal counsel must be at the table to negotiate any arrangements that affect the claims and lives of Survivors and their families.

With respect to the compensation provided to Japanese Canadians in 1980 for being interned during World War II, the government provided compensation quickly even though they were not legally obliged to. At the time, Prime Minister Brian Mulroney said compensation was being provided for their being interned just because it was morally and ethically the right thing to do. We would like the current Prime Minister, Paul Martin, to follow the same principle in having the federal government deal with the Residential School issues. Indian Residential School Survivors should not be treated as second- or third-class citizens of Canada.

The above principles are what have guided the positions and actions of Spirit Wind, particularly in relation to the Government of Canada and the alternative dispute resolution. In May 2003, approximately three weeks after the current deputy minister of Indian Residential School Resolutions Canada, Mario Dion, assumed his current position, the spiritual leader of Spirit Wind, Melvin Swan, had the opportunity to meet with him and present our principles and position on the Residential School issue.

We also presented a number of concerns that we requested be incorporated in the ADR program. When the ADR was announced in November 2003, it was clear that none of our concerns were taken seriously. On November 7, 2003, a press release by Spirit Wind denounced the ADR program as a seriously flawed and deliberate attempt to avoid responsibility and limit liability to Survivors.

We are also very critical of the announced $1.7 million program that estimated approximately $750 million of that total for government administrative and legal costs. The limiting of compensation to only sexual and severe physical abuse was also criticized in our press release, because it creates division, excluding those who were emotionally and physically abused, not to mention the cultural genocide and loss of language and identity that was inflicted upon us.

Unfortunately, many of the concerns we raised have come to be proven as fact. The spending of $4 out of every $5 spent on the ADR to date on government administration is gross injustice and colossal waste of the taxpayers' money. A small handful of claims are being processed while the government is doing everything it can to tie up and fight claims through the court process. People are being re-victimized through the ADR process. I am glad that this hearing will be looking into these issues.

I'm also disgusted with the treatment some Survivors have been subjected to through the government ADR program. Two Survivors from Manitoba, Mrs. Flora Merrick, who you just heard from, and her stepdaughter Grace Daniels, who you also just heard from, are here to tell you their experiences of what the federal government and the government lawyers say is a fair and compassionate program. Mrs. Merrick is the wife of the deceased Angus Merrick, an Order of Canada recipient, and Mrs. Daniels is his daughter. Mrs. Merrick had the small award granted her by an adjudicator appealed by the federal government because it did not fall within the rigid guidelines of the ADR program, which they arbitrarily set. Mrs. Daniels' small award, which I'm now told was turned down, was limited because it was subject to an arbitrary cap set by the federal government.

I am convinced that the action taken against Mrs. Merrick and Mrs. Daniels are part of a strategy of the federal government to intimidate and frighten Survivors from pursuing claims. This is reinforced by the recently announced government intention to spend millions of dollars of taxpayers' money to hire private investigators to investigate the information provided by Survivors in the ADR process. On CBC radio I said that this amounts to them calling us liars. I am not disputing the need to verify claims, but the hiring of private investigators to probe into our lives is an invasion of our privacy and may prejudice the safety of others as alleged perpetrators are asked about those who have named them as abusers.

Another instance of overt and covert intimidation, in my opinion, is the request of Indian Residential Schools Resolutions Canada for those with a criminal record to obtain their CPIC records from the RCMP. To obtain these records a person must go in person to a central RCMP regional office, make a formal request, be fingerprinted, and pay approximately $115 for a copy of the records.

If these records are needed by the federal government, they could obtain these records themselves, as the declaration for the ADR application signed by the applicant grants this authority. To say the least, forcing someone to go through the process they require will demean and discourage a number of people. This is also great disincentive for Survivors to pursue their Residential School claims.

I would also like to mention the hiring of so-called form-fillers, who are aboriginal, by Indian Residential Schools Canada to supposedly help Survivors fill out ADR applications. It has been reported to us that in many cases they are dissuading Survivors from obtaining legal representation. We have been told that in many cases after signing up with the form-fillers and being promised quick and substantial settlements, many of the ADR applicants are left to fend for themselves. In Manitoba we have been advised by Survivors that they have been told that their white lawyers will take their money and leave them with little of their ADR settlements.

Remember that the ADR program is currently only open to those over 70 years of age and to those who are in failing health. It is disgraceful that the federal government is hiring our own people to, in my words, lead our people like lambs to slaughter. It is clear that their intentions and actions are not in the best interests of Survivors, but intended to divide and conquer us. They are only after limiting the financial settlements to Survivors, regardless of their legal and administrative costs.

I have been advised that in many ADR hearings, two or three government lawyers and at least one federal case manager are present to protect the interests of the government. For them to actively discourage and dissuade Survivors to have competent legal representation is clearly unfair and a travesty of justice.

This committee should look into the government program and the hiring and the actions of these government-paid form-fillers. We must be assured that they are not misleading and ultimately hurting vulnerable Survivors who are enticed and convinced to sign with them.

All of the above and other actions of the federal government, in my opinion, prove that they cannot be trusted. Spirit Wind strongly supports the Baxter national class action as an option to deal with the estimated over 12,000 Residential School claims. Recently I had the pleasure of signing a memorandum of understanding pledging our support for the national class action. The recent certification of Ontario Mohawk class actions through the Cloud decision by the Ontario Court of Appeal, I am advised, will set the precedent for national class actions. However, this action, which will be important in bringing potentially timely and fair resolutions to Survivor claims, is being challenged by the Government of Canada. I'm advised they have recently asked the Supreme Court of Canada to overturn the Cloud decision. It is clear that the extent the government will go to control and limit the process and prevent a viable legal resolution to Residential School claims knows no bounds.

Many of us Survivors are elderly, in poor health, and many have died while waiting for justice. Unfortunately, it looks like many of us will die before our claims are dealt with. Those who have died should not have their claims die with them, as the government claims they will. They claim that they do not have any legal obligation to recognize these claims. What about the moral and ethical obligations to deal with these claims and the intergenerational claims they also refuse to recognize? It is disgraceful that they are being rewarded for delaying and avoiding dealing with Residential School claims. They must not be allowed to solve their Residential School legacy problem by waiting until all of us are dead. On behalf of Spirit Wind, I implore this committee not to let this happen.

Thank you very much.

APPENDIX G

Assembly of Manitoba Chiefs Resolution, Manitoba First Nations Children and Youth Class Action Lawsuit, August 2008

ASSEMBLY OF MANITOBA CHIEFS
20th ANNUAL GENERAL ASSEMBLY
BROKENHEAD OJIBWAY NATION
AUGUST 12, 13 & 14, 2008

CERTIFIED RESOLUTION

AUG-08. 04

RE: MANITOBA FIRST NATIONS CHILDREN & YOUTH CLASS ACTION LAWSUIT ON INDIAN RESIDENTIAL SCHOOLS CANADA (IRSC)

Moved by:
Chief Chris Baker
O-Pipon-Na-Piwin
Cree Nation

Seconded by:
Chief Murray Clearsky
Waywavseecappo
First Nation

CARRIED

WHEREAS, the Anishinabe, Inniwak, Dakota, Oji-Cree and Dene children and youth of our First Nation communities in Manitoba have been stripped of their right to our language and culture; and

WHEREAS, the Anishinabe, Inniwak, Dakota, Oji-Cree and Dene people have been directly affected and impacted by the Indian Residential Schools and the current Indian Education system by the lack of comprehensive language program funding; and

WHEREAS, the federal government has failed in their fiduciary responsibility to the First Nation children and youth of Manitoba in ensuring access to a quality education including language and culture programming in our schools; and

WHEREAS, the federal government has allocated 5 billion dollars to address the impacts and affects of the issue of Residential School compensation and that no monies have been allocated to our children and youth to learn, retain and preserve their ancestral languages; and

WHEREAS, the Assembly of First Nations National Chief delivered a passionate speech on the Residential School Compensation Package but failed to outline any long-term strategy for current and future generations in enhancing and preserving our languages and culture; and

WHEREAS, the Manitoba First Nation language teachers and educators are working in partnerships to develop language materials and teaching methods to teach the youth our languages with little or no funding; and

WHEREAS, the Chiefs of Manitoba have repeatedly passed supporting resolutions at Chiefs' Assemblies for the federal government to provide adequate funding for language and culture revitalization for our children and youth.

THEREFORE BE IT RESOLVED, that the Assembly of Manitoba Chiefs provide support for the Manitoba First Nation children and youth to launch a class action lawsuit against the federal government for language and cultural genocide as a result of the Indian Residential Schools Canada; and

FURTHER BE IT RESOLVED, that the class action lawsuit be named the Indian Residential Schools Canada lawsuit against Canada for compensation for our children and youth in the preservation of our languages and culture.

CERTIFIED COPY
of a resolution adopted
on August 12, 13 & 14, 2008
Brokenhead Ojibway Nation, Manitoba

Grand Chief Ron Evans

Assembly of Manitoba Chiefs Resolution, Continued Support for Spirit Wind, August 2009

ASSEMBLY OF MANITOBA CHIEFS
21ST ANNUAL GENERAL ASSEMBLY
NISICHAWAYASIHK CREE NATION
AUGUST 25, 26 & 27, 2009

CERTIFIED RESOLUTION

AUG-09.11

RE: CONTINUED SUPPORT FOR SPIRIT WIND INC.

Moved by:
Chief Glenn Hudson
Peguis First Nation

Seconded by:
Chief Gilbert G. Andrews
God's Lake First Nation

CARRIED

WHEREAS, The Chiefs-In-Assembly passed Resolution JAN-03. 15: "Support of the Spirit Wind Former Residential School Claimants Association"; and

WHEREAS, The Chiefs-In-Assembly subsequently passed Resolution MAY-03.22: "Support for the Strategy and Position of Spirit Wind Association for Survivors of the Indian Residential School System"; and

WHEREAS, 'Spirit Wind Inc.' (Spirit Wind) is now promoting the issue of recognition of the negative impact of "Day Schools" on First Nations Victims and Survivors; and

WHEREAS, Spirit Wind Inc. has promoted the issue(s) of compensation for First Nations Victims and Survivors including an official apology; and

WHEREAS, Spirit Wind has initiated a Class Action Law Suit on behalf of First Nation Victims and Survivors of Day Schools; and

WHEREAS, Spirit Wind is requesting political support but not financial support from the Assembly of Manitoba Chiefs (AMC) in its pursuit of addressing the Day School abuses of First Nations students in Manitoba.

THEREFORE BE IT RESOLVED, That the Chiefs-In-Assembly direct the AMC Grand Chief to support and acknowledge Spirit Wind Inc.'s intent in addressing the issue of abuse in Day Schools.

CERTIFIED COPY
of a resolution adopted on
August 25, 26 & 27, 2009
NISICHAWAYASIHK CREE NATION, Manitoba

_____

Grand Chief

NOTES

Preface

1 Shawn Wilson, *Research Is Ceremony: Indigenous Research Methods* (Halifax: Fernwood Publishing, 2008), 32. In addition, Teresa Marsh, Sheila Cote-Meek, Pamela Toulouse, Lisa M. Najavits, and Nancy L. Young have explained, "Within most Indigenous communities, researchers identify themselves at the beginning of the research: who we are, where we are from, and who our ancestors are. This transparency helps to establish trust." Teresa Marsh, Sheila Cote-Meek, Pamela Toulouse, Lisa M. Najavits, and Nancy L. Young, "The Application of Two-Eyed Seeing Decolonizing Methodology in Qualitative and Quantitative Research for the Treatment of Intergenerational Trauma and Substance Use Disorders," *International Journal of Qualitative Methods* 14, no. 5 (2018): 4.

Chapter One

1 Tape 1, 7:00–7:45.
2 Tape 1, 8:03–8:28.
3 Raymond Mason, "Spirit Wind Mission Statement," presented to Assembly of Manitoba Chiefs, 22 May 2003, 1–8.

Chapter Two

1 Tape 4, 12:15–12:52.
2 In 1988, Japanese Canadians were issued a formal apology by the prime minister of Canada, Brian Mulroney, for the wrongful internment of 22,000 Japanese Canadians during the Second World War. The apology and ensuing compensation for "symbolic redress payment of 21,000 dollars each" to the 13,000 remaining Survivors fulfilled an election promise from 1984. The $300 million settlement came one month after the United States also offered compensation for the wrongful internment of Japanese Americans during the same period. The settlement was intended to be one that "healed" and Prime Minister Mulroney stated, "We cannot change the past. But we must, as a nation, have the courage to face up to these historical facts." Peter Mansbridge, "1988: Government Apologizes to Japanese Canadians," CBC Digital Archives Video, 1–4:30, 22 September 1988. http://www.cbc.ca/archives/entry/1988-government-apologizes-to-japanese-canadians.
3 Tape 1, 9:04–9:37.

4 In Stephen Harper's official apology for children who suffered in residential schools, he stated in his opening paragraph that "Two primary objectives of the residential school system were to remove and isolate children from the influence of their homes, families, traditions, and cultures, and to assimilate them into the dominant culture. These objectives assumed Aboriginal cultures and spiritual beliefs were inferior and unequal. The phrase 'to kill the Indian in the child' actually originated as the phrase 'Kill the Indian, save the man' from American captain Richard H. Pratt, who became the first superintendent of Carlisle Indian Industrial School, one of the most influential in North America. Today, we recognize that this policy of assimilation was wrong, has caused great harm, and has no place in our country." Stephen Harper, Canada, Parliament, Aboriginal Affairs and Northern Development Canada, *Statement of Apology to Former Students of the Indian Residential School*, 11 June 2008. http://www.aadnc-aandc.gc.ca/eng/1100100015644/1100100015 649; Official Report of the Nineteenth Annual Conference of Charities and Correction (1892), 46–59. Reprinted in Richard H. Pratt, "The Advantages of Mingling Indians with Whites," *Americanizing the American Indians: Writings by the "Friends of the Indian" 1880–1900* (Cambridge: Harvard University Press, 1973), 260–71.

5 Tape 4, 25:01–25:20.

6 In addition to the cultural genocide attempted by the residential schools, the "Sixties Scoop" played an important role in removing Indigenous children from their families in Canada. An estimated 20,000 children were removed from their homes in this period. The Truth and Reconciliation Commission of Canada notes in its final report that "by the end of the 1970s, the transfer of children from Residential Schools was nearly complete in southern Canada, and the impact of the Sixties Scoop was in evidence across the country. In 1977, Aboriginal children accounted for 44% of the children in care in Alberta, 51% of the children in care in Saskatchewan, and 60% of the children in care in Manitoba." Truth and Reconciliation Commission of Canada, *Canada's Residential Schools: The History, Part 2 1939–2000* (Montreal & Kingston: McGill-Queen's University Press, 2015), 172–3. Cindy Blackstock has stated that today, "Canada's inequitable funding policy ... contributes to more First Nations children being in state care than at the height of residential schools." The impacts of government policies, past and present, are ongoing. Cindy Blackstock, "Residential Schools: Did They Really Close or Just Morph into Child Welfare?" *Indigenous Law Journal* 6 (2007): 71.

7 A report from the Office of the Correctional Investigator in 2013 demonstrated that, although Aboriginal people constitute approximately 4 percent of the Canadian population, "as of February 2013, 23.2% of the federal inmate population is Aboriginal (First Nation, Métis or Inuit) ... the incarceration rate for Aboriginal adults in Canada is estimated to be ten times higher than the incarceration rate of non-Aboriginal adults." Government of Canada, Office of

the Correctional Investigator, *Aboriginal Offenders – A Critical Situation*, 9 September 2013. http://www.oci-bec.gc.ca/cnt/rpt/oth-aut/oth-aut20121022 info-eng.aspx.

8 The connection between residential schools and an increased number of Indigenous adults in prison was well noted on the first page of the introduction to the Truth and Reconciliation Legacy findings: "The disproportionate apprehension of Aboriginal children by child welfare agencies and the disproportionate imprisonment and victimization of Aboriginal people are all part of the legacy of the way that Aboriginal children were treated in Residential Schools." Truth and Reconciliation Commission of Canada, *Canada's Residential Schools: The Legacy* (Montreal & Kingston: McGill-Queen's University Press, 2015), 3.

9 The effects of these institutions are still hurting First Nations communities. Aboriginal Affairs identified in 2012 "a series of issues undermining the effectiveness of the Enhanced Prevention Focused Approach: complex medical needs, the high cost of institutional care, an increase in older children coming into care, housing shortages and overcrowding, shortages of Aboriginal foster parents, lack of program supports for parents with addiction or mental health problems, and poverty. Aboriginal Affairs noted agencies report that some families are unable to meet their basic needs (food, fuel for heating, transportation to medical appointments, etc.) and find themselves unable to care for their children." Truth and Reconciliation Commission, *The Legacy*, 24.

10 Indeed, residential schools were built illegally on Indigenous lands by the Government of Canada. To visualize these schools, see https://www.aadnc-aandc. gc.ca/eng/1290453474688/1290453673970. In a distinct form of land acknowledgment, public school boards, such as Canada's largest, the Toronto District School Board, recognize the Indigenous land on which school buildings have been erected.

11 Criteria for the inclusion of residential schools were based on these factors: "a) The child was placed in a residence away from the family home by or under the authority of Canada for the purposes of education; and, b) Canada was jointly or solely responsible for the operation of the residence and care of the children resident there. (3) Indicators that Canada was jointly or solely responsible for the operation of the residence and care of children there include, but are not limited to, whether: a) The institution was federally owned; b) Canada stood as the parent to the child; c) Canada was at least partially responsible for the administration of the institution; d) Canada inspected or had a right to inspect the institution; or, e) Canada did or did not stipulate the institution as an IRS. (4) Within 60 days of receiving a request to add an institution to Schedule 'F,' Canada will research the proposed institution and determine whether it is an Indian Residential School as defined in this Agreement and will provide both the Requestor and the NAC with: 64 a) Canada's decision on whether the institution is an Indian Residential School; b) Written reasons for

that decision; and c) A list of materials upon which that decision was made; provided that Canada may ask the Requestor for an extension of time to complete the research." Indian Residential School Settlement Agreement, 8 May 2006, 63–4. http://www.residentialschoolsettlement.ca/IRS%20Settlement%20Agreement-%20ENGLISH.pdf.

This resulted in day school survivors as well as other claimants being unable to access the lawsuit. Teulon Indian Residential School Survivors were recently denied their appeal from the Supreme Court after the Manitoba courts denied them access to the agreement. The Canadian Press, "Supreme Court Refuses to Hear Appeal in Manitoba Residential School Case," *National Post*, 17 August. https://nationalpost.com/pmn/news-pmn/canada-news-pmn/supreme-court-refuses-to-hear-appeal-in-manitoba-residential-school-case.

12 Tape 4, 15:03–15:55.
13 Ibid., 16:49–17:32.
14 Ibid., 18:08–18:41.
15 Finding a lawyer who would help Indigenous people for free was a difficult task at first due to the seemingly impossible goal of winning compensation. The TRC found, "Throughout the civil litigation period, many Residential School Survivors were unable to afford the legal fees required to file suit against the federal government. As a result, individual Survivors were usually required to access legal services on a contingency basis, which meant that they would not pay their lawyers unless they were successful in obtaining compensation. In most Residential School litigation, the contingency fee arrangements provided that lawyers would receive at least 30 percent of any compensation awarded to the Survivors." Luckily for Spirit Wind, as explained above, Dennis Troniak had a personal connection to the schools and offered to help Raymond Mason free of charge until a settlement had been reached. Truth and Reconciliation Commission, *The Legacy*, 208.
16 Tape 4, 18:58–19:50.

Chapter Three

1 Saulteaux Chief Peguis (1774–1864) was originally from the Great Lakes region but moved west to settle south of Winnipeg in the last decade of the eighteenth century. During the early nineteenth century, his people helped Selkirk settlers to survive. The settlers had emigrated from Scotland through a deal with the Hudson Bay Company to protect its interests against their rivals of the North West Company. Then, "in 1817 Peguis finalized western Canada's first treaty with Lord Selkirk, ceding land along the Red River. He became a Christian in 1840 and was baptized 'William King' ... [but] disenfranchisement with European settlement set in in the 1860s after Peguis watched newcomers illegally push onto Native land." Beginning in the late 1890s, the village of East Selkirk, as well as the town of Selkirk and the rural municipalities of St

Clements and St Andrew's began incorporating the lands of the reservation and taxing the white occupants who held patents to river lots. This began a dispute that ultimately led to the 1907 relocation of the Saulteaux to a remote corner of Lake Winnipeg to join the Peguis Reserve. Peguis First Nation finalized a land claim in 2008 that originated from this incident. Thomas Thorner and Thor Frohn-Nielsen, *A Few Acres of Snow: Documents in Pre-Confederation Canadian History* (Toronto: University of Toronto Press, 2009), 291.

2 In 1871, Mason's great-grandfather (Henry Prince), signed Treaty 1, which provided a reserve for Indigenous peoples north of Winnipeg called St Peters Reserve. See https://web.archive.org/web/20111014140158/http://www.aadnc-aandc.gc.ca/eng/1100100028664/1100100028665. This was one year after Manitoba entered Confederation. "The Peguis First Nation (or St Peters Reserve at the time) was entitled to the allocation of land for its Reserve based on 160 acres for each family of five, or 32 acres per person. However, it was also expressly agreed that land already occupied and improved by the First Nation members was not to be included in the calculation of Treaty land entitlement." This wish was not fulfilled and, without settling the dispute, Canada surrendered the land in 1907 relocating the band 190 km north of Winnipeg. This dispute was brought to court and has been ongoing throughout the 1980s and 1990s and recently, in 2010, the government began paying members of the band who lost title to these lands. The overall settlement obligated "Canada [to] pay Peguis the sum of $64,425,000 ... entitlement to approximately 260 square miles (166,794 acres) of additional Reserve land and a $5 million community fund to compensate Peguis for Canada's delay." Peguis First Nation, *Review: Negotiation of a Settlement Treaty Entitlement of Peguis First Nation*, Newsletter No. 8, May 2006. http://www.peguisfirstnation.ca/wp-content/uploads/2015/10/tle_3.pdf.

3 Tape 1, 15:00–15:17.

4 Ibid., 15:30–15:39.

5 Ibid., 20:44–21:21–21:49.

6 Tuberculosis was the largest cause of death for Indigenous students in the period between 1940 and 2000 accounting for nearly 40 percent of all recorded deaths in residential schools. The system was chronically underfunded by the director of Indian Affairs, Dr Harold McGill, who had announced in 1937, "as part of a cost-cutting effort, there would be no funding for tuberculosis surveys or for treatment in sanitaria or hospitals for First Nations people suffering from chronic tuberculosis. This policy was eventually stopped due to pressure from anti-tuberculosis societies but by 1944, the department was still short roughly 1,500 beds for Indigenous tuberculosis patients. In 1949, the problem got so severe, the federal government made a tuberculosis plan for Manitoba and x-rayed First Nation students annually. Within six years, the tuberculosis rate was only a tenth of what it had been in the 1940s." Truth and Reconciliation Commission, *The History, Part 2 1940 to 2000*, 190–5.

7 Tape 1, 19:00–19:40. While, at this time, Ray was unable to speak English, by the time he left residential school, he could no longer speak Ojibway.

8 Ibid., 16:01–16:49.

9 Tape 4, 1:15:40–1:16:35.

10 The residential school actively used corporal punishment as a method of discipline embedded within religious contexts; "discipline in schools was based in scripture: corporal punishment was a biblically authorized way of keeping order and of bringing children to the righteous path." Moreover, "in many cases, residential schools imposed punishments on Aboriginal children that were in excess of the norms that would be accepted even in Euro-Canadian society at that time." Truth and Reconciliation Commission of Canada, *Canada's Residential Schools: The History, Part 1 Origins to 1939* (Montreal & Kingston: McGill-Queen's University Press, 2015), 519–20.

11 In 1894, the federal government put in place regulations regarding the residential school system. Under the new rules, attendance for Indigenous students was voluntary. However, if an "Indian agent or justice of the peace thought that any 'Indian child between six and sixteen years of age is not being properly cared for or educated, and that the parent, guardian, or other person having charge or control of such child, is unfit or unwilling to provide for the child's education,' he could issue an order to place the child 'in an industrial or boarding school which there may be a vacancy for such child.'" Moreover, if a child was placed in the care of a residential school, they could not be discharged without department approval. To enforce these actions truancy or police officers and sometimes representatives from the Department of Indian Affairs could obtain a warrant to search any building if they suspected a student was not attending school. Phil Fontaine, Aimée Craft, and Truth and Reconciliation Commission of Canada, *A Knock on the Door: The Essential History of Residential Schools from the Truth and Reconciliation Commission of Canada* (Winnipeg: University of Manitoba Press, 2016), 36.

12 Tape 1, 22:01–22:36.

13 Helen Raptis writes, "Residential schools [were] grounded in the discourse of liberalism, with its emphasis on individual attainment. Thus, siblings were purposely segregated to discourage linguistic and cultural retention and to promote each child's absorption into Canadian social mores. Many children developed a hatred for their families, and consequently, for themselves, making return to their homes difficult." Helen Raptis, *What We Learned: Two Generations Reflect on Tsimshian Education and the Day Schools* (Vancouver: University of British Columbia Press, 2016), 30.

14 Tape 1, 23:01–23:12.

15 Ibid., 23:18–23:30.

16 Ibid., 23:32–23:45.

17 Ibid., 24:10–24:29.

18 Ibid., 25:33–25:55.

19 Ibid., 26:00–26:30.

20 Birtle Residential School opened in 1888 as a partnership between the Can-
    adian government and the Presbyterian Church. Overcrowding, disease, and
    failing infrastructure would create a number of problems for the school at-
    tendance, which ranged from nineteen to 170 depending on the year. The
    school was operational for eighty-one years and severe levels of physical, emo-
    tional, and sexual abuse are well documented in the TRC. Victoria McAuley,
    Birtle School, 17 August 2018. https://presbyterianarchives.ca/2018/08/17/
    birtle-school/.

21 Tape 1, 31:33–32:34.

22 The federal government implemented a funding plan in 1957 that was sup-
    posed to provide the residential schools with budgets in order to supply "the
    students with nutritionally adequate diets and sufficient supply of clothing."
    However, during "a meeting of United Church and Presbyterian Church school
    principals with Indian Affairs officials in Winnipeg in 1964, Birtle, Manitoba,
    school principal M. Rusaw said that the 'older children, especially boys who
    are really young men need so much more food than we can provide. They are
    constantly hungry.'" Truth and Reconciliation Commission, *The History, Part 2
    1940 to 2000*, 295. Many students throughout the system went hungry and this
    led to severe health issues since they were not provided with the nutrients
    for proper growth in childhood. The Truth and Reconciliation findings re-
    ported that "the federal government knowingly chose not to provide schools
    with enough money to ensure that kitchens and dining rooms were prop-
    erly equipped, that cooks were properly trained, and most significantly that
    food was purchased in sufficient quantity and quality for growing children
    … This can be seen only as a massive failure to provide the essentials needed
    for health, and a deep betrayal of Canada's responsibility to children as their
    primary caregivers while the children were in the institutions to which they
    were assigned." Ibid., 299; Tape 1, 33:55–34:17.

23 Tape 1, 32:27–33:25: While Mason referred to various abuses over the course
    of our conversations, it was extremely difficult for him to talk about events
    that contained abuse in his childhood. He had previously recounted them
    in excruciating detail during his Independent Assessment Process in 2008
    where he believed that would be the last time he had to recall these mem-
    ories. He told the adjudicator that he "had hoped that the hearing would 'be
    the end of it, but he knows that he still has some healing to do.'" He wanted to
    "shut the door on this legacy" (Appendix B). Due to that fact, we did not ask
    Mason to explain any further details regarding instances of abuse. We have
    agreed to include the ruling of the Independent Assessment Process, which
    was presided over by Anne M. Wallace, Q.C. That process explicitly laid out
    the types and manner of abuses that occurred and has been formally accepted
    into the Indian Residential School Agreement granting Mason compensation
    for these crimes. Since this story intends to tell Mason's truth from his own

perspective, it includes his allegations, not the Canadian government's, and shows the ruling of Wallace (Appendix B). Per our ethical agreement, names of abusers have also been removed. For more information regarding how this process was conducted, please see chapter 4 and Indian Residential Schools Adjudication Secretariat. http://www.iap-pei.ca/home-eng.php.

24 Running away from residential schools was a common event among First Nation students who felt disenfranchised with the treatment they were receiving. However, the Department of Indian Affairs made sure that students who did run away would be pursued by all legal, and extra-legal, means in order to bring them back. For example, "even without warrant, Indian Affairs employees and constables had the authority to arrest a student in the act of escaping from a residential school and return the child to school." Fontaine, Craft, and Truth and Reconciliation Commission, *A Knock on the Door*, 36. There are multiple testimonies about children running away from residential schools and particularly Birtle in every decade of its operation. However, escaping and getting caught meant harsh punishment and abuse, which usually meant that the students suffered more punishment when they were returned to the school. For example, the Presbyterian-run residential school in northwestern Ontario, Cecilia Jeffrey, is infamously known as the school from which Chanie Wenjack escaped, dying in the attempt. The official inquest into his death found that the principal "said the strapping punishment was instituted as a corrective measure for students who run away." The principal was Colin Wasacase, who had previously attended Birtle and Portage la Prairie as a student, both of which Mason would experience a decade later. Truth and Reconciliation Commission, *The History, Part 2 1940 to 2000*, 343.

25 Tape 1, 34:38–38:53.

26 In her autobiography, Verna Kirkness, an Indigenous teacher from Fisher River Cree Nation who was allowed to teach at Birtle Residential School because she was not considered an Indigenous person under the Indian Act, described the strict segregation of genders. She wrote that, "as was typical in the Residential Schools of the day, the boys and girls were segregated to a ridiculous degree. Even Brothers and Sisters regardless of age did not get to spend time together." Verna J. Kirkness, *Creating Space: My Life and Work in Indigenous Education* (Winnipeg: University of Manitoba Press, 2014), 31.

27 The TRC details a number of students who either ran away, got severely sick, went hungry, were injured in work accidents, were arrested for theft or truancy, or were physically abused while attending Birtle Residential School. The moniker "scrapper" would have been appropriate as Mason struggled with finding his place in this type of atmosphere. Truth and Reconciliation Commission, *The History, Part 2 1940 to 2000*, 137–9, 336–5, 356–8, 367, 374, 383. This school's reputation for being difficult even when compared to other residential schools is also clear in the autobiography of Verna Kirkness. She wrote, "instead of being happy to have an Indian teacher with whom the

children could identify, the administrations tried to discourage them from spending time with me ... I wondered if they were afraid the children would tell me things about their lives away from the classroom ... It was my first real negative school experience that impacted my life as an Indian person. I knew something about Residential schools, but being there and seeing children who were away from their parents and communities, sensing their loneliness and what I perceived as unfair treatment made me uneasy." In addition, after one egregious incident, she contacted the Women's Missionary Society to complain about the treatment of the children. She left two years later, and her assessment of the school's conditions reveal even more about the character of the institution. She explained that "if I had been a high-school student there, I surely would not have been able to tolerate the regime, or the repressive and confining atmosphere, and either would have dropped out as many did or would have been expelled for breaking one of the many rules." Kirkness, *Creating Space*, 29–33.

28 The Department of Indian Affairs wanted to increase the number of Indigenous students attending schools among integrated areas. In the department's 1961 report, they explained that the "integration of Indians into Canada's wage economy continues to be faced with such basic problems as a general lack of education, suitable work skills, orientation to the non-Indian community, and the necessary motivation to make the transition." Pursuing this goal led to the integration in the Portage la Prairie Agency and "caused the closing of the one remaining classroom at the Portage Indian Residential School and of two classrooms at the Brandon Indian Residential School, which brought the total in attendance at city schools at Portage la Prairie and Brandon to 129 and 85 respectively." Indian Affairs Annual Report, Department of Citizenship and Immigration (Ottawa: Queen's Printer, 1961), 6, 85.

29 Tape 1, 41:51–42:40.

30 Student abuse of fellow students was a commonly reported experience at residential schools throughout the country. As of 30 September 2013, one-third of admitted IAP (Independent Assessment Process for compensation for Residential Schools) claims, or 8,470 of the 26,261 admitted IAP claims were related to the abuse of students by students. The TRC noted that these were a "serious and widespread problem" among the schools that was not adequately handled by school officials. Truth and Reconciliation Commission, *The History, Part 2 1940 to 2000*, 410–11.

31 Tape 1, 45:49–45:59.

32 Ibid., 48:10–51:46.

33 Ibid., 52:33–53:10.

34 The TRC determined only "one recorded prosecution for the abuse of Residential School students in Manitoba. In 2005, a person who had attended the Dauphin school in the early 1960s and worked there in the late 1960s as a supervisor was convicted of indecently assaulting seven Dauphin students.

He was sentenced to two years less a day." Truth and Reconciliation Commission, *The History, Part 2 1940 to 2000*, 430.

35 In 1955, two of the former schools used by the Presbyterian Church were in such disrepair they needed to be closed. The government was supposed to offer another institution in northern Manitoba but built a new school in Dauphin, Manitoba, centrally located and only 300 kilometres northwest of Winnipeg. Truth and Reconciliation Commission, *The History, Part 2 1940 to 2000*, 60. The residential school officially opened in 1957 with 200 students but expanded throughout the 1960s adding dormitories so that students could attend high school classes in town. The school officially closed in 1969 but continued to provide a dormitory for students who wanted to take classes in town. *Mackay School – The Pas, MB and Dauphin, MB.* Compiled by General Synod Archives, 23 September 2008, http://www.anglican.ca/tr/histories/mackay.

36 Tape 1, 1:01:48–1:02:39.

37 Ibid., 56:16–57:00.

38 Ibid., 57:45–59:05. Athletics and sporting events were a key part of "civilizing" Indigenous men in residential schools into English culture. The TRC discusses the various sports that were played and quotes a 1911 *Globe and Mail* article that argued, "Sport is a fundamental essential not only of English life but also of human life itself, and the question that confronts us today is this – upon what can we better build up and establish the character and physique of the future builder and maintainer of the Empire than upon the foundation of sport in its highest and noblest form?" Truth and Reconciliation Commission, *The History, Part 1 Origins to 1939*, 361.

39 Tape 1, 1:00:09–1:01:29.

Chapter Four

1 Tape 2, 0:39–3:19.

2 The city of Thompson, Manitoba is essential to Raymond's story as it is the first place he arrives after leaving the residential school. The historical context of this city and the seemingly boundless opportunities presented to Mason need to be described to help readers understand the culture of this remote community. Located approximately 750 kilometres north of Winnipeg, the city was created in a joint partnership with the provincial government and the International Nickel Company, Ltd (INCO) in 1956, upon the discovery of a significant ore deposit that could produce 75 million pounds nickel or nearly 20 percent more for the company, per year. Within fourteen years the population had risen from zero to over 25,000 as INCO invested 175 million dollars into constructing a processing facility, and an entirely new city equipped with a modern hospital, houses, and schools. Graham Buckingham describes the period: "If there were a category in 'the Guinness Book of World Records' for

the most quickly developed town, then Thompson, Manitoba would probably hold first place forevermore. The speed the growth of the town took place is typified by the year 1957. In this particular year everything seemed to be happening at once." INCO operations at this site officially began in the 1960s and in the first year of that decade increased "the total value of all our [Manitoba's] metal production to three times what it was in 1960." Perhaps even more striking were the comments Buckingham made about Thompson during the years he would arrive. He writes, "the development of Thompson can, perhaps, best be likened to the development of a child. By 1962 the childhood years were over and the period between 1962 and 1966 were adolescent years, the 'who am I?' years, the years when Thompson sought its identity as a community and its independence from 'mother' INCO." Mason's life was on a similar trajectory as he sought his identity in this remote yet prosperous region and gained independence from the paternalist residential schools, entering a town without limits in the mid-1960s. Graham Buckingham, *Thompson, a City and Its People* (Thompson, MB: Thompson Historical Society, 1988), 1, 21, 30, 100, 121.

3 Tape 2, 3:29–3:42.

4 Ibid., 4:40–4:48.

5 Ibid., 5:26–5:52.

6 Ibid., 13:33–14:08.

7 The legacy of these schools has repeatedly illustrated that addiction developed among First Nations populations as a way to cope with lasting impacts of abuse. Moreover, "due in large part to the Residential schools, Aboriginal people in Canada are more likely to have experienced the types of risk factors associated with addiction." In addition, many survivors described a "lack of self-esteem, alcoholism, domestic violence, marriage break down and lack of parenting skills." Truth and Reconciliation Commission, *The Legacy*, 153, 194.

8 Tape 2, 5:58–6:45.

9 Ibid., 15:10–16:10.

10 Ibid., 16:33–17:14.

11 Ibid., 17:18–22:20.

12 Ibid., 23:31–23:54.

13 Indigenous people also have a much higher rate of incarceration when compared to off reserve crime as a result of the residential schools. The TRC found that "although some Aboriginal people have been wrongfully convicted of crimes that they did not commit, most are in jail for having committed some offence. The available evidence suggests that these offences are likely to be violent and are likely to involve alcohol or other drugs. Over half of those who had been convicted had been convicted of assault or sexual offences or driving offences, 24.2% had been convicted of theft, 11.3% had been convicted of drug offences, 8.1% had been convicted of robbery, and 4.8% had been convicted of murder." Moreover, it was found that "we must understand the reasons why

those affected by the intergenerational legacy of Residential Schools commit crimes if we are to reduce offences among Aboriginal people and the growing crisis of Aboriginal overrepresentation in prison." Truth and Reconciliation Commission, *The Legacy*, 220.

14 Tape 2, 23:58–25:00.

Chapter Five

1   Tape 2, 38:42–38:58.
2   On 1 February 1968, one of the most important events of Canada's military history took place when the law that eliminated the Royal Canadian Navy, the Royal Canadian Air Force, and the Canadian Army went into effect, and the three proud military services ceased to exist. Daniel Gosselin, "Hellyer's Ghosts: Unification of the Canadian Forces Is 40 Years Old – Part One," *Canadian Military Journal* 9, no. 2 (2008): 6.
3   Tape 2, 40:38–40:56.
4   A recent report obtained by the CBC and prepared by the Defence Aboriginal Advisory group for the commander of the Canadian Army, Lt.-Gen. Marquis Hainse, stated, "we strongly believe there is a systemic issue within the Department of National Defence (DND) and Canadian Armed Forces (CAF) that is rampant throughout all ranks and elements of Land, Air Force and Navy and this issue is serious enough that an external review is imminent." The report also stated that "this is not the military our Aboriginal members signed up for and this is not the military they dedicated their lives to. Victims are being forced out of the military, yet the aggressors continue on – some excelling at their careers." Mason's account of his life in the Armed Forces echoes these sentiments that must have been developing throughout the Canadian military prior to 2017. Ashley Burke, "Report Condemns 'Systemic' Racism toward Indigenous Military Members | CBC News, 13 December 2016. http://www.cbc.ca/news/canada/ottawa/canada-military-indigenous-racism-report-1.3891862.
5   Tape 2, 41:52–41:29.
6   Ibid., 42:33–44:18.
7   Ibid., 44:19–44:33.
8   Ibid., 44:40–45:25.
9   Ibid., 45:29–45:47.
10 Indigenous history is intimately linked with the Canadian military as Indigenous people have served in all major wars that the country entered since before Confederation. However, during the residential school period from the 1870s to 1996, the cadet system and military at large were used for similar assimilative purposes. Evan Habkirk's review of the cadet portion of the military found that state officials found "these [military] activities were believed to be effective tools for replacing Indigenous identities rooted in a separate nationhood with a commitment to the Canadian state, curbing wayward

habits, inculcating a work ethic that aligned with the needs of industrial style production, and engaging them in military preparedness. Evan J. Habkirk, "From Indian Boys to Canadian Men? The Use of Cadet Drill in the Canadian Indian Residential School System," *British Journal of Canadian Studies* 30, no. 2 (2017): 228.

11   Tape 2, 45:55–47:15.

12   In 2001, a study conducted by Dr Charles Barfield determined that students who attended residential schools would experience post-traumatic stress disorder with a constellation of symptoms known as the residential school syndrome. He wrote, "the Residential School syndrome diagnosis is different from that of post-traumatic stress disorder in that there is a significant cultural impact and a persistent tendency to abuse alcohol or other drugs that is particularly associated with violent outbursts of anger ... As might be the case for anyone attending a boarding school with inadequate parenting, parenting skills are often deficient. Strikingly, there is a persistent tendency to abuse alcohol or sedative medication drugs, often starting at a very young age." Charles Barfield, "Residential School Syndrome," *British Columbia Medical Journal* 43, no. 2 (2001): 78–81.

13   Tape 2, 47:03–47:34.

14   Ibid., 47:46–48:09.

15   Mason referred to God and Providence here. He opted to not talk about this extremely difficult period in his life on tape as he has done so before during his testimony in the Independent Assessment Process. With the permission of Mason, the rest of this paragraph is phrased from that document's proceedings. Indian Residential Schools Resolution Canada, *Independent Assessment Process, Report of Decision-Maker on Behalf of Claimant Raymond Mason*, E-S442-10aM-00487, 18 July 2008, Winnipeg, Manitoba, 9. The ramifications of abuse negatively impacted the mental health of Indigenous peoples. The TRC explained, "sexual and physical abuse, as well as separation from families and communities, caused lasting trauma for many others. In many cases, former students could find no alternatives to self-harm. The effects of this trauma were often passed on to the children of Residential School Survivors and sometimes to their grandchildren. The overall suicide rate among First Nation communities is about twice that of the total Canadian population." Truth and Reconciliation Commission, *The Legacy*, 7.

16   The name of Raymond Mason's first wife has been changed to fit with our ethical agreement. We struggled about the role that these narratives regarding Raymond's personal relationships should play in this history. At first, Raymond wanted to keep them in the manuscript, but changed his mind over the course of the writing. We have redacted these names to honour Raymond's past personal relationships.

17   Raymond attending post-secondary is against the odds for Indigenous peoples whose rate of enrolment is disproportionally low for their population. For

example, "statistical records showed that, in 1996, there was an estimated 54% drop-out rate for Aboriginal students compared to the 35% of the general population." Therefore, roughly 50 percent of the population would not be allowed to apply for university due to the fact they did not complete a high school degree. Tracey King, "Fostering Aboriginal Leadership: Increasing Enrollment and Completion Rates in Canadian Post-Secondary Institutions," *College Quarterly* 11, no. 1 (2008): 7. By the early 2000s, the number of Indigenous post-secondary students was still only a shocking 6 percent of the population. Jane Preston, "The Urgency of Postsecondary Education for Aboriginal Peoples," *Canadian Journal of Educational Administration and Policy* 86 (2008): 12.

18   Tape 1, 28:28–30:51

19   Tape 2, 50:04–50:48.

20   Again, the name of Raymond Mason's second wife has been changed to fit with our ethical agreement.

21   Mason's story of success and then failure was also shared by other survivors as they were released from residential schools. The TRC found "theirs is a story of marginalization and lost opportunity. The Residential Schools graduated few role models and mentors. The poor-quality education led people into chronic unemployment or underemployment. Beyond that, it led to levels of poverty, poor housing, substance abuse, family violence, and ill health." Truth and Reconciliation Commission, *The Legacy*, 61–2.

22   Elder Edmund Metatawabin's story about his residential school experience parallels Mason's and further supports the continuing trauma experienced by survivors. Metatawabin demonstrates how his marriage broke up repeatedly due to his returning to alcohol. He also lost a good job at Trent University due to alcohol. Like Mason, Metatawabin has told his story in collaboration with another person, author and journalist Alexandra Shimo. The author's note in this book states, "I was hampered by gaps in my memory, perhaps because of my unusual childhood or the trauma of what I would later do to my body. In July 2011, I began to work with author and journalist Alexandra Shimo to try to close those gaps. She interviewed people from my past, and dug up old court transcripts, St Anne's Residential School records, police interviews and reports through Freedom of Information requests, photos and news articles to fill in those places where my memory was spotty, checking them against my own recollections." Edmund Metatawabin and Alexandra Shimo, *Up Ghost River: A Chief's Journey through the Turbulent Waters of Native History* (Toronto: Vintage Canada, 2012), xiii.

23   Tape 2, 58:54–59:13.

24   Ibid., 59:40–1:00:28.

25   Ibid., 1:00:58–1:01:15.

26   The sentencing of Indigenous people in Canada's justice system has usually resulted in larger proportions of the population being incarcerated. However, in this case the judge recognized that Mason was trying to get his life back

together and provided him an opportunity to correct his behaviour. Some decisions have recognized that abuses suffered in the residential schools were a contributing factor towards crimes that occurred after they were released. The TRC found that "in R. v. Craft, the accused received a nine-month conditional sentence and three years' probation for driving under the influence. Chief Judge Ruddy of the Yukon Territorial Court made very explicit connections to Residential School: His time spent in the Residential School system was an extremely difficult period of time in which he, as is described in the report, suffered from extreme violence, torture and sexual abuse within the Residential School system. That, in turn, led to him abusing alcohol, which in turn led to his extensive involvement with the criminal justice system between 1961 and 1986." Truth and Reconciliation Commission, *The Legacy*, 230–1.

27   Tape 2, 1:02:05–1:02:28.

28   Mental health problems are listed as one of most enduring legacies of the residential school abuses and a significant reason why intergenerational effects of the institutions still negatively impact Indigenous peoples. In fact, "Many former students told the Commission that they were denied the opportunity to learn nurturing parenting skills and they replicated the strict and uncaring discipline that they experienced at school. The lack of positive strategies for dealing with interpersonal conflict may have led to high rates of family breakdown and problems that youth carry with them into their adult lives." Truth and Reconciliation Commission, *The Legacy*, 155.

29   Tape 2, 1:02:45–1:04:12.

30   Ibid., 32:28–33:10.

31   Tape 4, 58:15–59:18.

32   Tape 2, 36:31–37:09.

33   Ibid., 37:10–37:33.

34   Today, Peguis First Nation is located 190 km north of Winnipeg, Manitoba and has a population of 2,704 Indigenous people living on the reserve with a mixed background of Cree and Ojibwa descent. Statistics Canada, *Peguis 1b, Indian Reserve, Manitoba Census Profile*. Census subdivision by Government of Canada Statistics, 2016.

Chapter Six

1   During the official investigation into the residential schools in 2005, Dennis Troniak testified in the House of Commons that "it has always been puzzling to me that instead of vigorously pursuing a policy of comprehensive national settlement, reconciliation, and healing in the face of one of the greatest human rights injustices in our history, involving the destruction of tens of thousands of families and horrendous damage to the lives of hundreds of thousands of children, the Government of Canada hides behind legalisms and platitudes.

One of the greatest stories of courage, of the strength of spiritual light over darkness, and of the victory of the human spirit over adversity is told in the lives of the Survivors. Many of those lives ended in squalor and abject misery, and we are stricken by that knowledge. Many, however, including witnesses you heard Tuesday and will hear from today, are testimonies to triumph in the face of adversity that we who have not lived their experience can scarcely imagine ... The government continues to deny them justice as it unconscionably tries to defend the indefensible. So, I ask the Prime Minister today, and ask the members of his cabinet and his caucus, and ask any parliamentarian who stands in the way of justice on this issue, 'Have you no shame? Have you no shame?'" Canada. Parliament. Standing Committee of Aboriginal Affairs and Northern Development. *Evidence*. 1st Sess, 38th Parliament, 17 February 2005. http://www.ourcommons.ca/DocumentViewer/en/38-1/AANO/meeting-19/ evidence.

2 Tape 2, 1:06:06–1:07:34.

3 Ibid., 1:08:41–1:09:27.

4 Ibid., 1:09:28–1:09:49.

5 Evidence of D.C. Scott to the Special Committee of the House of Commons Investigating the Indian Act Amendments of 1920 (L–2) (N–3), RG10, volume 6810, file 470-2-3, volume 7, Library and Archives Canada.

6 Tape 2, 1:10:40–1:10:53.

7 Ibid., 1:11:58–1:12:07.

8 The term "cultural genocide" is used throughout this text as an important finding from Spirit Wind's Elders and was embedded within several of the attached claims for justice. This term also had complex legal interpretations that have been highlighted by political scientists David. B MacDonald and Graham Hudson, who explained, "genocide has different interpretations among academics, domestic courts, international tribunals, and victimized people." Moreover, MacDonald "argued that 'cultural genocide' or 'ethnocide' may be appropriate as a ground floor to describe much of Canada's treatment of Aboriginal peoples and is often used by genocide scholars. This is employed when mass death did not accompany colonization, but where we see active attempts to destroy culture." David B. MacDonald and Graham Hudson, "The Genocide Question and Indian Residential Schools in Canada," *Canadian Journal of Political Science/Revue canadienne de science politique* 45, no. 2 (2012): 445, 422. MacDonald further explained in 2015, "In promoting the academic term cultural genocide, it has virtually eliminated the possibility of a large-scale denialist movement ... has stayed within its mandate, and has been able to cement the approval of Survivors." David B. MacDonald, "Canada's History Wars: Indigenous Genocide and Public Memory in the United States, Australia, and Canada," *Journal of Genocide Research* 17, no. 4 (2015): 414, 426.

9 Since Canada is a member of the United Nations, it is supposed to follow numerous conventions and declarations. For example, "The preamble of the

United Nations *Convention on the Rights of the Child* states that to ensure that a child has the opportunity for 'the full and harmonious development of his or her personality, [he or she] should grow up in a family environment, in an atmosphere of happiness, love and understanding.' In safe and secure homes, children can be 'brought up in the spirit of the ideas proclaimed in the Charter of the United Nations, and in particular in the spirit of peace, dignity, tolerance, freedom, equality, and solidarity.'" In addition, in 2007, the United Nations entrenched these rights with the *Declaration on the Rights of Indigenous Peoples*, which also "prohibited the forcible removal of Indigenous children to other groups." Truth and Reconciliation Commission, *The Legacy*, 30.

10 Tape 4, 20:56–22:10.

11 The TRC found several attempts by the Canadian government to minimize the damage of these institutions. In one case, "the Attorney General of Canada had considerable success with so-called 'crumbling skull' arguments. These arguments assert that while the Survivors experienced difficulties in their lives, these difficulties were not sufficiently related to being sexually abused in the schools to be compensable. The argument was that Survivors were already damaged before they came to the schools. They had 'crumbling skulls' and would have experienced difficulties, such as unemployment, addictions, and imprisonment, even if they had not been abused in the schools." Moreover, several courts "were reluctant to recognize claims that Survivors made seeking compensation for loss of family, language, and culture. Often these claims were dismissed on the basis that they had been brought too late and that statute of limitation defences applied to these claims, in a way that they did not apply to claims of sexual and sometimes serious physical abuse." Truth and Reconciliation Commission, *The Legacy*, 204–6.

12 Tape 4, 34:48–35:40.

13 Tape 2, 1:12:47–1:13:

14 Raymond Mason, "Spirit Wind Strategy Presentation," Annual Assembly of Manitoba Chiefs Meetings, 23 May 2005.

15 Ibid.

16 Ibid.

17 Kim Lunman, "Lawyers Praised for Support of Native Survivors," *Globe and Mail*, 17 August 2004, 5.

18 Ibid.

19 Ibid.

20 Ibid.

21 Ibid.

22 Raymond was unsure about where this grant was from but after doing more research, we found that it was connected to the Advocacy and Public Information Program Partners (APIP) as part of the Settlement Agreement. The site lists Spirit Wind as receiving $25,000 in 2008, $50,000 in 2009, but another

payment of $141,169 in 2007. This money was part of a $28 million package with 140 First Nations organizations to inform survivors about the agreement (section 3). https://www.aadnc-aandc.gc.ca/eng/1291389942185/1291390155707.

The payments continued for some organizations until 2014 but Spirit Wind's stopped in 2009–10 or the time they started hosting meetings for day school Survivors. In addition, a 2009 study found the "lack of clarity in the program's expected results and performance measurement gaps severely inhibit the Program's capacity to monitor performance, measure the achievement of expected results, or identify issues or factors which may differentially affect access to information to and participation in benefits from the Settlement Agreement. These gaps have also severely limited the evaluation's capacity to assess expected results and cost-effectiveness."

See http://www.aadnc-aandc.gc.ca/eng/1100100011737/1100100011742.

23 Ibid.

24 As a result of the number of cases brought forth from the end of the 1990s to the early 2000s, Jennifer Llewellyn has argued that the Canadian government wanted to settle residential school lawsuits out of court, stating, "the logjam caused by the sheer volume of cases in the courts will cost Canadian governments huge sums of money in court administration costs. Additionally, the government is faced with mounting costs for their legal defence and compensation awards. The churches have recently warned of impending bankruptcies or serious financial problems as a result of their legal costs and potential compensation awards. These problems have prompted calls from all the parties involved for the development of alternatives means of addressing Residential School abuses." Jennifer J. Llewellyn, "Dealing with the Legacy of Native Residential School Abuse in Canada: Litigation, ADR, and Restorative Justice," *The University of Toronto Law Journal* 52, no. 3 (2002): 263–4.

25 Tape 4, 27:50–29:58.

26 Mason, "Spirit Wind Strategy Presentation," Annual Assembly of Manitoba Chiefs Meetings, 23 May 2005.

27 The Truth and Reconciliation *Legacy Report* explains the ADR process by using the case of Flora Merrick, who was one of the original members of Spirit Wind as referenced by Mason. The report states that in 2005 the House of Common's Standing Committee on Aboriginal Affairs and Northern Development heard from Flora Merrick, "an eighty-eight-year-old Elder whose $1,500 ADR award was being appealed by the federal government. The issue was whether she should be compensated for 'being strapped so severely that my arms were black and blue for several weeks' and for being 'locked in a dark room for about two weeks' after she ran away from Portage la Prairie Residential School. Merrick explained that she was willing to accept the $1,500 award, not as a fair and just settlement, but only 'due to my age, health, and financial situation. I wanted some closure to my Residential School experience, and I could

use the money, even as small as it was. I am very angry and upset that the government would be so mean-spirited as to deny me even this small amount of compensation … I'm very upset and angry, not only for myself, but also for all Residential School Survivors.'" The committee recognized the urgency of the matter and noted that "on average some 30 to 50 former students die each week uncompensated and bearing the grief of their experience to the grave." The committee agreed unanimously, and in very strong terms, that the ADR process was a denial of justice, concluding that it "regrets the manner with which the Government has administered the Indian Residential Schools Claims program" and that the ADR process should be terminated. It recommended that "on an urgent basis, with consideration for the frailty and short life expectancy of the former students," the federal government should move to court-supervised negotiations with former students to secure a court-approved settlement." Truth and Reconciliation Commission, *The Legacy*, 213.

28   See below for a full description of the Alternative Dispute Resolution.

29   Canada. Parliament, Standing Committee of Aboriginal Affairs and Northern Development. *Evidence*. 1st Sess, 38th Parliament, 17 February 2005. The Truth and Reconciliation Report notes that Ruth Roulette's testimony contains phrasing similar to this speech, but Mason is adamant that it was translated by her on behalf of Grace Daniels (her mother). Truth and Reconciliation Commission, *The History, Part 2 1939–2000*, 566. http://www.ourcommons.ca/DocumentViewer/en/38-1/AANO/meeting-19/evidence.

30   Debbie O'Rourke, "The Forgotten Scandal: Feds Lavish Millions on Lawyers while Fleecing Residential School Victims," *NOW Magazine*, 28 April 2005, https://nowtoronto.com/news/the-forgotten-scandal/.

31   Kathleen Mahoney recounts a similar experience in her review of the ADR process. She writes, "My client was the late Dennis Fontaine from the Skageeng First Nation in Manitoba, the brother of the national chief. In taking up Mr Fontaine's case, it was necessary for me to carefully study the process that had led him to Ottawa. I learned that he was a participant in one of the pilot projects that were launched in Manitoba to 'test run' the ADR process. After examining the elements of the pilot, I was most disappointed to discover that the guiding principles derived from the national dialogues had been largely ignored in the implementation of the pilot projects as well as in the creation of the ADR process. Survivors, including Dennis Fontaine, felt they were being re-victimized and betrayed." Kathleen Mahoney, "The Settlement Process: A Personal Reflection," *The University of Toronto Law Journal* 64, no. 4 (2014): 509. http://www.jstor.org/stable/24311939.

32   O'Rourke, "The Forgotten Scandal." https://nowtoronto.com/news/the-forgotten-scandal/.

33   Ibid.

34   Ibid.

35   Ibid.

36 The Truth and Reconciliation Report also notes the failure of the entire ADR process, explaining, "the process was criticized for having been developed without the consultation or input of Survivors, for failing to be impartial and even-handed, for limiting compensation to an excessively narrow class of Survivors, and for the slow pace at which it provided compensation. It was also noted that the ADR was 'strikingly disconnected from the so-called pilot projects that preceded it.' The following month, the Supreme Court of Canada issued a decision that allowed Survivors to pursue class-action lawsuits for Residential School damages. The repudiation of the ADR program, coupled with the prospect of large-scale class-action suits, forced the government and the churches back to the negotiating table." Truth and Reconciliation Commission, *The History, Part 2 1939–2000*, 566.

37 Tape 4, 31:36–31:55.

38 The Truth and Reconciliation Report stated, "One of the most significant criticisms was that applicants did not always automatically receive the full amount of compensation to which they were entitled … Canada paid 70% of the award to Survivors from Catholic-run schools. To recover the other 30%, Survivors would have to initiate separate court action against the appropriate Roman Catholic entities." Truth and Reconciliation Commission, *The History, Part 2 1939–2000*, 565; Tape 4, 30:02–30:49.

39 The entire ADR process has resulted in horrific results for Indigenous peoples who agreed to partake in the agreements. Kathleen Mahoney again explains, "the limited goals of the ADR resulted in serious inadequacies. The narrow range of compensation coverage, the unequal treatment of Survivors, the lack of healing or truth telling components as well as the overall de-contextualized approach failed to come to grips with what Survivors had clearly indicated they wanted from the process. This was especially true with respect to the loss of language, culture, and family life that most if not all Survivors experienced. In its 2003 performance report, even the government department created for the resolution of Residential School claims raised red flags warning that the ADR process risked re-victimizing claimants. Nonetheless, government officials proceeded to create a compensation plan that was discriminatory, unequal, and unfair." Mahoney, "The Settlement Process: A Personal Reflection," 510.

40 The Cloud Action case refers to Marlene Cloud who in 1988 claimed $2.3 billion for survivors of the Mohawk Institute in Brantford, Ontario, which was operated by the federal government, Anglican Church, and the New England Company, for the "sustained, systemic program of physical, emotional, spiritual, and cultural abuse they suffered. Cloud and the other Survivors claimed damages for a breach of fiduciary duties, breaches of the Family Law Act, loss of culture and language, and breach of Treaty and Aboriginal rights." Truth and Reconciliation Commission, *The Legacy*, 207. The Baxter case refers to "Charles Baxter Sr, Elijah Baxter, and others [who in 2000] filed a class-action

lawsuit against the federal government in the Ontario Superior Court. The statement of claim sought damages for negligence, breach of statutory duties under the Indian Act, and breach of Treaty obligations. Since it included claims on behalf of students who attended Residential Schools throughout Canada, it was often referred to as the 'national class action.' Over time, Survivor associations and litigants from around the country joined the Baxter class-action suit." Ibid., 270. The Blackwater case refers to the Supreme Court case in 2005 of Blackwater v. Plint that emerged from British Columbia's survivors against the Untied Church who operated schools in the region between the 1940s and the 1960s. Blackwater v. Plint, [2005] 3 S.C.R. 3, 2005 SCC 58.

41 Kim Lunman, "Lawyers Praised for Support of Native Survivors," *Globe and Mail*, 17 August 2004, 5.

42 Baxter v. Canada (Attorney General) (2006), 83 o.r. (3d) 481 (O.S.C.J.) at para 4.

43 Ibid. During the 1990s, a change in the law allowed survivors to use class-action lawsuits against the government in Ontario and British Columbia. The other provinces would follow suit by 2003, as this type of lawsuit allowed "one part [to] sue as a representative of a larger 'class' of people. Such suits are seen to serve a public benefit because they reduce overall costs by eliminating the need for repetitive hearings, allow for greater access to the courts, and can modify the behaviour of actual and potential wrongdoers." Truth and Reconciliation Commission, *The Legacy*, 207.

44 The TRC found that these two cases were instrumental in bringing about a national class action settlement. It writes, "In October 2001, Justice Roland J. Haines of the Ontario Superior Court declined to certify the Cloud case, saying that the experiences of the students were too diverse to constitute a representative class, that many of the claims would be barred by statute of limitations provisions, and that the plaintiffs failed to establish that a class action suit was the preferable procedure for their claims. The decision was upheld by the Ontario Divisional Court. In December 2004, however, the Ontario Court of Appeal overturned the earlier rulings and certified the Cloud case. The Court of Appeal stressed that class actions were preferable to individual actions because they would increase 'access to justice.' This was a very important decision and the Supreme Court's refusal to hear an appeal of this decision played an important role in encouraging the government and the churches to settle all of the claims through a national class action settlement agreement." Ibid., 207–8.

45 Tape 4, 45:50–46:29.

46 Ibid., 47:02–47:42.

47 The Truth and Reconciliation Report also notes that Spirit Wind, "the largest Manitoba Survivor association, entered into a memorandum of understanding with the National Consortium to support the Baxter national class action in 2005." Truth and Reconciliation Commission, *The History, Part 2 1939–2000*, 568.

48 Tape 4, 48:05–48:53.

49 "After the Ontario Court of Appeal's decision in Cloud was released in December 2004, the parties in the Baxter had a case conference with Justice Warren Winkler of the Ontario Superior Court to set a timetable for the certification motion. During the case conference, it became clear that as a result of the third-party claims against the churches, significant evidentiary issues had emerged, which threatened to significantly delay the proceedings. On 30 May 2005, Justice Winkler refused to hear preliminary arguments about the third-party claims, and directed the certification motion to be heard first. The motion was never heard, since, in the subsequent months, Aboriginal organizations, church organizations, and the federal government entered into talks that would lead to the Indian Residential Schools Settlement Agreement." Truth and Reconciliation Commission, *The History, Part 2 1939–2000*, 570. "In 2006, the parties agreed to merge the existing class-action suits into a single class action in each of the nine jurisdictions in which they had been originally led (British Columbia, Alberta, Saskatchewan, Manitoba, Ontario, Quebec, Yukon, Nunavut, and the Northwest Territories). This action would be referred to as 'Fontaine v. Canada (Attorney General).' In this case, Phil Fontaine acted as the representative plaintiff on behalf of all former Residential School students and the AFN." Ibid., 572.

50 Ibid.

51 The Truth and Reconciliation Report notes, "since it included claims on behalf of students who attended Residential Schools throughout Canada, it was often referred to as the 'national class action.' Over time, Survivor associations and litigants from around the country joined the Baxter class-action suit." Truth and Reconciliation Commission, *The Legacy*, 207.

52 The Truth and Reconciliation Report stated that in 2003 the Baxter case originally tried to sue Canada and individual churches but later focused on the federal government exclusively. It further explained, "In response, on April 24, 2003, Canada brought a claim against the churches, arguing that they were responsible for the day-to-day operation of the schools, and named eighty-five separate church institutions. In addition to the Cloud and Baxter class-action suits, seventeen other class actions were filed in nine provinces and territories during this time." Truth and Reconciliation Commission, *The History, Part 2 1939–2000*, 569.

53 Baxter v. Canada (Attorney General) (2006), 83 o.r. (3d) 481 (O.S.C.J.) at para. 13–21. Jeremy Patzer also writes, "by the time the Baxter class action was being settled in 2006 – the settlement that ultimately became the Indian Residential Schools Settlement Agreement – Residential Schools were the subject of around fifteen thousand ongoing claims in Canadian courts." Jeremy Patzer, "Residential School Harm and Colonial Dispossession," in *Colonial Genocide in Indigenous North America*, ed. Andrew John Woolford, Jeff Benvenuto, and Alexander Laban Hinton (Durham: Duke University Press, 2014), 176.

54 Darcy Merkur would write to Raymond in 2016, explaining, "Spirit Wind was instrumental in the early stages of the class action. At that time, we needed grassroots support for the litigation and the closure that it could help bring. Spirit Wind was that grassroots organization that helped kickstart the settlement initiative … We genuinely believe that Spirit Wind was instrumental in increasing the pressure on the Government of Canada to respond to the litigation and help resolve the Residential School claims through the National Class Action settlement that was ultimate achieved."

55 John Milloy explained that the AFN chief (Phil Fontaine) organized "the initial discussions that led eventually to the Settlement Agreement." These discussions "were held between [Paul] Martin and [Phil] Fontaine when they travelled together to attend the Pope's funeral in Rome." The AFN would continue negotiations until an agreement was reached. John Milloy, "Doing Public History in Canada's Truth and Reconciliation Commission," *The Public Historian* 35, no. 4 (2013): 13.

56 Mason is referring to the Common Experience Payment (CEP) that was issued in the Indian Residential School Settlement Agreement. Mayo Moran explains that the agreement "mandated a 'Common Experience Payment' (CEP) to be paid to every eligible Survivor of Residential Schools covered by the Agreement. The CEP recognizes the experience of residing at an Indian Residential School and its impacts and does not require the showing of additional harms beyond the fact of attending an included IRS. Former students of included schools receive $10,000 for the first school year and $3,000 for each subsequent year. The CEP program received over 105,000 applications of which more than 78,000 were found eligible. The average payout per recipient was just over $20,000. The total CEP payout to date is $1,664 billion." Mayo Moran, "The Role of Reparative Justice in Responding to the Legacy of Indian Residential Schools," *The University of Toronto Law Journal* 64, no. 4 (2014): 532. http://www.jstor.org/stable/24311940; Paul Barnsley, "AFN Launches Class Action Lawsuit," *Windspeaker Publication* 23, issue 6, (2005): 8. http://ammsa.com/publications/windspeaker/afn-launches-class-action-lawsuit.

57 Ibid.

58 In Kent Roach's review of the Canadian law system that determined the Indian Residential School Settlement Agreement processes, he writes, "Canadian law blames the victim when it encourages and often accepts causation-based crumbling skull arguments. Canadian law blames the victim when it deducts time spent in prison from damages for the loss of future earnings caused by abuse at Residential Schools. Finally, Canadian law blames the victims when trial judges dismiss the relevance of the legacy of Residential Schools when sentencing Aboriginal offenders, especially those who have suffered the intergenerational harms that the schools have inflicted on Aboriginal families and communities." In addition, Roach is pessimistic about the way the Canadian law system helps Indigenous people, finding "fundamental limitations in the

ability of the Canadian legal system, even at its most flexible and generous, to recognize and respond to the harms of Residential Schools and perhaps other historical and collective wrongs … Canadian civil and criminal law should confront and redress its continuing re-victimization of Aboriginal people harmed by Residential Schools." Kent Roach, "Blaming the Victim: Canadian Law, Causation, and Residential Schools," *The University of Toronto Law Journal* 64, no. 4 (2014): 595.

59 The Independent Assessment Process (IAP) was "an adjudicative process created by the Agreement to award compensation for serious harms, including physical and sexual abuse. Administered by an independent Adjudication Secretariat, the IAP was designed to be a fair and impartial claimant-centred adjudication process. Over one hundred adjudicators work in this process, which is headed by the Chief Adjudicator. The Chief Adjudicator is advised by the Oversight Committee. The original projection suggested that the IAP would receive approximately 12,000 to 15,000 claims. In fact, by the 19 September 2012 deadline, over 37,000 applications had been received. As this article goes to press, more than 20,098 hearings have been held and over $2.275 billion in compensation has been awarded. Moran, "The Role of Reparative Justice," 533. Mayo Moran was the chair of the Oversight Committee for IAP, so her perspective is in some ways subjective. Kent Roach has disputed the claim that the IAP was fair, arguing, "nevertheless, they discount the fact that the CEP payment received by close to 79,000 Survivors averaged out to under $20,000, based on a formula of $10,000 plus $3,000 for every year proven to have been spent in a Residential School. Even the average IAP payment for sexual and serious physical abuse amounts to just under $115,000 per person, including legal costs. The individual assessment process established by the settlement attempted to avoid adversarial excess, but it also incorporated Canadian causation law with respect to the most serious consequential harms. It did not, for example, instruct adjudicators to resolve difficult causation issues by reference to the numbered treaties, which generally guaranteed on-reserve schools as desired by the Aboriginal groups, or to Aboriginal law." Roach, "Blaming the Victim," 569.

60 Roach has also noted that "the modest nature of the common experience payments provided to all former students reflected the unwillingness of Canadian courts to recognize claims related to treaty violations and to loss of language, culture, and family attachment." Ibid., 568-9.

61 Alexandra Paul, "Lawyer Mortgaging Land to Repay Clients," *Winnipeg Free Press*, 6 May 2011, 4.

62 Ibid.

63 Roach reinforced the role that Indigenous Survivors needed to play in order for their IAP claims to be heard, arguing "even if crumbling skull arguments were not always accepted by judges, they ensured that the entire life of Survivors, from their earliest family life to any errors they made in their own lives,

would be subject to adversarial discovery and trial. It is a testament to the courage and probably also the anger of the Survivors that so many of them were prepared to run this victim-blaming gauntlet in these lawsuits." Roach, "Blaming the Victim," 593. More troubling is John Milloy's explanation that "to add insult to injury, it is well known that many Survivors did not receive the full amount of compensation that they deserved because it could not be established by the government that the claimant had attended school for the number of years she or he contended. In many such cases, the final decision went against the claimants even though it has been established that the government began cycles of file destruction beginning in the Second World War and that that process included Indian Affairs files, specifically quarterly reports, used to certify attendance." Milloy, "Doing Public History," 12.

64 "Alleged Perpetrators and the Independent Assessment Process (IAP)," Indian Residential Schools Adjudication Secretariat, n.d. http://www.iap-pei.ca/faq-eng.php?act=factsheets/perpetrators-eng.php.

65 Ibid.

66 Ibid.

67 "Private Eyes to Look for Alleged Residential School Abusers," CBC News, 29 November 2013. https://www.cbc.ca/news/canada/manitoba/private-eyes-to-look-for-alleged-Residential-school-abusers-1.2446143.

68 Through a review of the IAP process, Roach also found that "almost 38,000 former living students have applied under the 2006 settlement for compensation for serious physical or sexual abuse. This number dwarfs the handful of criminal prosecutions against alleged abusers in the schools. The lack of prosecutions can only partially be explained by the age of the cases: police and prosecutors were often unwilling to prosecute in the absence of corroborating evidence and some victims were unwilling to make formal complaints. Some of the prosecutions re-victimized complainants, as the accused successfully sought disclosure of all of their medical and employment record." Roach, "Blaming the Victim," 567. As outlined by Mason's IAP in Appendix B, he did not want to undergo a medical assessment to prove crimes committed fifty years earlier. The adjudicator notes for Mason's case that "while the application claims harm level five, the claimant's counsel advised after the person of interest hearing that the claimant did not wish to undergo an assessment because of the further time that would be required to complete the process. The claimant has restricted his claim under this heading to harm level three."

Chapter Seven

1 Archival evidence has revealed that Methodist Indian day schools played a significant role in helping the Canadian government assimilate Indigenous peoples in the northern regions of Manitoba. Moreover, the typical curriculum

would be Eurocentric, as Susan Elaine Gray explains: "The emphasis in day schools was on providing students with a suitable English education. If the government was to build Canadian citizens (or, at least, citizens coming as close to the Euro-Canadian ideal as one could come) one of the best ways to begin was with a good solid English Canadian education in the schools. From 1867 to 1900, therefore, reading, spelling, arithmetic, grammar, history, geography, music, singing, and drawing were taught in Indian day schools. Some emphasis was placed on fine arts. This was important as it was believed that a truly educated person was in possession of a broad range of accomplishments. In some day schools, advanced students were taught catechism, dictation, mental arithmetic, composition, and Scripture, and were given object lessons. The education of the spirit was an important part of Canadianizing any Indian, just as it was for training any Euro-Canadian or immigrant student." Susan Elaine Gray, "Methodist Indian Day Schools and Indian Communities in Northern Manitoba, 1896–1925," *Manitoba History 30 (1995)*: http://www.mhs.mb.ca/docs/mb_history/30/methodistdayschools.shtml.

2   Tape 4, 1:00:40–1:01:48.

3   The loss of language was perhaps the most damaging form of cultural genocide enacted by institutions of this nature. An entire chapter in the TRC's final report, entitled "'I lost my Talk': The Erosion of Language and Culture," depicts reasons why state officials attempted to eradicate their languages. At the time, "Indian Affairs appears to have had no other policy on the use of language in the schools beyond its requirement that English and French were to be the only two languages of instruction and the only two languages to be taught in the schools. The government simply thought the languages were disappearing and would be of no interest or value to Aboriginal children in the future." This was especially damaging, as Elder Eli Taylor explained: "Embodied in Aboriginal languages is our unique relationship to the Creator, our attitudes, beliefs, values, and the fundamental notion of what is truth ... Language is the principal means by which culture is accumulated, shared, and transmitted from generation to generation. The key to identity and retention of culture is one's ancestral language." Truth and Reconciliation Commission, *The Legacy*, 155.

4   "Justice for Indian, Inuit, Metis Day Schools Survivors," *Turtle Island Native Network*, 6 April 2011. http://www.turtleisland.org/discussion/viewtopic.php?f=4&t=8467&sid=ac38ea469aa2cd9d197a13d132450c53.

5   The TRC notes the dissatisfaction with the way the settlement was completed. Although Spirit Wind did not support the efforts of the AFN led by Phil Fontaine, Fontaine himself offered similar sentiments when asked about the agreement. "In his affidavit filed in support of the settlement, [Fontaine] described how his mother, Agnes Mary Fontaine, was taken from her family when she was seven years old and forced to attend Fort Alexander Residential School from 1919 to 1928. He described how his mother 'suffered by being removed from the care of her parents, family, and community, and not being

allowed to speak her native language, or practice traditional spiritual ways. She also suffered sexual, physical and emotional abuse, and was given inadequate food, health care and education. Chief Fontaine, who acted as the executor of his mother's estate after she died in 1988, recognized that 'it is tragic that so many have died during this fight to have the wrongs that were perpetuated on Aboriginal people through Residential Schools acknowledged.'" Truth and Reconciliation Commission, *The Legacy*, 214.

6 Spirit Wind obtained support from the Assembly of Manitoba Chiefs for their efforts for day school Survivors in 2009.

7 While not all First Nations people practise the sweat lodge ceremony, the Ojibway nation, to which Ray Mason belongs, does. Marsh, Marsh, Ozawagosh, and Ozawagosh discuss the effectiveness of sweat lodges in their article "The Sweat Lodge Ceremony: A Healing Intervention for Intergenerational Trauma and Substance Use." They argue that "Elders teach that the sweat lodge ceremony serves a sacred purpose through the ritual healing or cleansing of body, mind, and spirit while bringing people together to honour the energy of life (personal communication Elders Julie and Frank Ozawagosh, 5 January 2013). The Elders teach that each person enters the lodge with his or her own challenges, suffering, conflicts, addiction, and concerns. This sitting together brings connection, truth, harmony, and peace through sweating, praying, drumming, sharing, stories, and singing." T.N. Marsh, D.C. Marsh, J. Ozawagosh, F. Ozawagosh, "The Sweat Lodge Ceremony: A Healing Intervention for Intergenerational Trauma and Substance Use," *The International Indigenous Policy Journal*, 9, no. 2 (2018): 1–22.

8 Tape 3, 4:25–5:05.

9 "Aboriginal Day School Survivors File $15B Lawsuit," *CTV News*, 5 August 2009. https://www.ctvnews.ca/aboriginal-day-school-survivors-file-15b-lawsuit-1.422733.

10 Ibid.

11 Ibid.

12 Ibid.

13 Ibid.

14 Tape 3, 6:58–7:42.

15 Ibid., 7:47–7:55.

16 Gowling WLG is still the lead law firm in the 2009 filing of "Aboriginal Day School Class Action: Garry Leslie McLean, Roger Augustine, Angela Elizabeth Simone Sampson, Margaret Anne Swan, and Mariette Lucille Buckshot v Her Majesty The Queen." The firm now represents fifteen different First Nations and is continuing to seek compensation from the federal government in a class action lawsuit. If any person reading this footnote has experienced abuse at the Indian day schools and would like to register with the class action, Gowling WLG website asks you to contact the toll free number: 1 (844) 539–3815, or email Christian Ruest at christian.ruest@gowlingwlg.com. GowlingWLG,

Aboriginal Day School Class Action. https://ca.gowling.wlg.com/dayschoolclassaction/.

17 Research into the day schools has shown that similar types of abuses occurred, but also that "the fragile state of almost all Aboriginal languages in Canada is a damaging legacy of Residential Schools. Although the schools contributed greatly to the decline, so too did the federal day schools and public schools, which made no room for Aboriginal languages or cultural expression. The repressive policies used against Aboriginal languages and cultures in all schools, and in Canadian society generally, were based on the view that Aboriginal languages and cultures were primitive, savage, and inferior." Truth and Reconciliation Commission, *The Legacy*, 137.

18 Gloria Galloway, "Court Approves Class-Action Lawsuit for Indigenous Students Who Say They Were Abused at Day Schools," *Globe and Mail*, 8 July 2018. https://www.theglobeandmail.com/canada/article-court-approves-class-action-lawsuit-for-indigenous-students-stripped/.

19 Ibid.

20 Ibid.

21 In her opening address, Minister Carolyn Bennett stated, "Today, we are here to recognize that a harm was done and to take another important step on our journey of reconciliation, together. Today, another truth will be told. Beginning in the 1920s close to 200,000 Indigenous children attended federally operated Indian Day Schools. Institutions where children went to school during the day and returned home at night. As a result of the harmful and discriminatory government policies at the time, students who attended these schools were subject to sexual, physical and psychological abuse and forced to abandon their language and culture. Survivors across this country continue to suffer from the abuse and horrible experiences they were subjected to, which was perpetuated by the very people charged with educating them as children. We, as a country, must admit where and when harm was caused, and today marks a historic step in that journey towards reconciliation and healing. Harm was caused by the system, put in place by the federal government, that has negatively impacted generations of First Nations, Inuit and Métis. Over the past several months the Government of Canada and the council for the plaintiffs have been engaged with negotiations to address the harms suffered in a fair, compassionate and respectful manner which balances individual compensation with forward-looking initiatives so survivors no longer need to rely on courts to obtain justice … We are investing $200 million to support healing, wellness, education, language, culture and commemoration for all those affected by Indian Day Schools. The Government looks forward to working with the plaintiffs to negotiate the details of this investment. The federal government of Canada will continue to negotiate with the plaintiffs to reach a final settlement." "Government Reaches Agreement with Former

Indian Day School Students." http://www.cpac.ca/en/programs/headline-politics/episodes/65894245.

22 Karen Pauls, "'Just Get It Done': Indian Day School Survivors Divided Over Proposed Settlement," *CBC News*, 14 May 2019. https://www.cbc.ca/news/canada/manitoba/just-get-it-done-indian-day-school-survivors-divided-over-proposed-settlement-1.5132262.

Chapter Eight

1 In June 2010, when the Truth and Reconciliation Commission held an event in Winnipeg on its cross-country mandate, Stephen Harper was the prime minister. A year earlier in 2009, Harper stated at the G20 summit in Pittsburgh that "we also have no history of colonialism." This remark, coupled with Ray's experience seeking compensation through the Independent Assessment Process and the ensuing lawsuit he would start in the same year on behalf of day school Survivors, indicates why he was unwilling to participate in the reciprocal reconciliation events. John Milloy, "Doing Public History in Canada's Truth and Reconciliation Commission," 13.

2 Tape 4, 13:52–14:34.

3 The Truth and Reconciliation Commission of Canada's ninety-four Calls to Action will be discussed later. These are accessible here: http://trc.ca/assets/pdf/Calls_to_Action_English2.pdf.

4 As a recent news report has found, "By the end of 2017, Canada had received applications for 1,531 distinct institutions to be added to the agreement. To date, all but nine of these institutions have been ruled ineligible ... There were an estimated 1,000 students who had boarded at the Teulon Residence. They had all been separated from their families and endured the same cultural whitewashing that other survivors had. Why should they be denied compensation?" Josiah Neufield, "Courts Tell Residential School Survivors They Didn't Go to a Residential School," *United Church Observer*, May 2018. https://www.ucobserver.org/justice/2018/05/Residential_school/.

5 Truth and Reconciliation Commission, *Calls to Action* (Winnipeg: Truth and Reconciliation Commission of Canada, 2015), 5.

6 In Helen Raptis's review of the Tsimshian Indigenous Day School in British Columbia, she reports similar types of experiences as outlined by the TRC. She writes, "Yet both the day schools prior to the Second World War and the public schools afterward also played important roles in eroding traditional Tsimshian learning and livelihood. Whether they were attending residential schools, day schools, or integrated public schools, Tsimshian students experienced the negative effects of ill-conceived government policies pertaining not only to schooling but also to the fabric of their individual and communal lives." Raptis, *What We Learned*, 152–3.

7   Tape 4, 50:48–51:33.
8   Mason, "Spirit Wind Strategy Presentation," Annual Assembly of Manitoba Chiefs Meetings, 23 May 2005.
9   Truth and Reconciliation Commission, *Calls to Action*, 7.
10 Ibid.

Chapter Nine

1   Tape 3, 13:33–13:54.
2   Tape 3, 9:45–10:15.
3   Tape 3, 11:44–12:09
4   Mason, "Spirit Wind Mission Statement," presented to Assembly of Manitoba Chiefs, 22 May 2003, 1–8. Rayond Mason's story reflects systemic over-representation of Indigenous peoples in Canadian's incarcerated population. See statistics from the Canadian Department of Justice, https://www.justice.gc.ca/eng/rp-pr/jr/jf-pf/2017/jan02.html, as well as (sporadic) editorial coverage, for example, here: https://www.cbc.ca/news/indigenous/indigenous-incarceration-justice-system-panel-1.4729192.
5   Assembly of First Nations Thirty-Ninth Annual Meeting, Vancouver, 25 July 2018
6   Tape 1, 39:33– 40:01.
7   Ibid.

Afterword

1   Truth and Reconciliation Commission, *Calls to Action* (Winnipeg: Truth and Reconciliation Commission of Canada, 2015), 7.
2   Ibid.
3   Provincial Committee of Aims and Objectives of Education in the Schools of Ontario, *Living and Learning: The Report of the Provincial Committee on the Aims and Objectives of Education in the Schools of Ontario* (Toronto: Ontario Department of Education, 1968), 1.
4   "Basic Principles for the College Programme, Faculty of Education 1965–1970," 1185.1 Faculty of Education, Box 1, Queen's University Archives.
5   Ibid.
6   Truth and Reconciliation Commission, *Calls to Action*, 8.
7   Truth and Reconciliation Commission, *The History, Part 1 Origins to 1939*, 585.
8   Ibid.
9   Truth and Reconciliation Mandate, *Schedule N of the Indian Residential School Settlement Agreement*, 1.
10 David Milward, "Justice Denied for Tina Fontaine and Colten Boushie: How Their Cases Illustrate Racism in Canadian Court," *CBC News*, 25 February 2018. https://www.cbc.ca/news/canada/manitoba/tina-fontaine-colten-boushie-justice-denied-1.4549469.

11 Renate Eigenbrod and Renée Hulan, *Aboriginal Oral Traditions: Theory, Practice, Ethics* (Halifax: Fernwood Publishing, 2008), 5.

12 Ibid.

13 Sylvia Moore, *Trickster Chases the Tale of Education* (Montreal & Kingston: McGill-Queen's University Press, 2017), 134.

14 Peter Geller, "Many Stories, Many Voices: Aboriginal Oral History in Northern Manitoba," *Oral History Forum* 23 (2003): 10.

15 Neal Mcleod, "Cree Narrative Memory," *Oral History Forum* 19–20 (1999): 38.

16 Laura Jane Murray and Keren Dichter Rice, *Talking on the Page: Editing Aboriginal Oral Texts* (Toronto: University of Toronto Press, 1999), xii.

17 Walter J. Ong and John Hartley, *Orality and Literacy: The Technologizing of the Word* (London: Routledge, Taylor & Francis Group, 2013), 168. Ong and Hartley note, "Writing created history. What did print do to what writing created? The fuller answer cannot be simply quantitative, in terms of increased 'facts.' What does the feeling for closure fostered by print have to do with the plotting of historical writing, the selection of the kinds of theme that historians use to break into the seamless web of events around them so that a story can be told? In keeping with the agonistic structures of old oral cultures, early history, though written, was largely the story of wars and political confrontation. Today we have moved to the history of consciousness."

18 Ibid., *Orality and Literacy*, 140–6.

19 Tape 2, 1:02:35–1:02:55

20 McGill-Queen's copy editor has also made changes to ensure that the text is consistent with the press's spelling and style guides.

21 Murray and Rice, *Talking on the Page*, xiv.

22 Georg Iggers was a well-known historian of historiography, but also a civil rights activist who fled with his Jewish family from Nazi Germany before the Second World War.

23 Georg G. Iggers, *Historiography in the Twentieth Century: From Scientific Objectivity to the Postmodern Challenge* (Middletown, CT: Wesleyan University Press, 2005), 160.

24 Scott Lauria Morgensen, "Destabilizing the Settler Academy: The Decolonial Effects of Indigenous Methodologies," *American Quarterly* 64, no. 4 (2012): 806, 808.

25 Pamela Palmater, "Decolonization Is Taking Back Our Power," in P. McFarlane and N. Schabus, eds, *Whose Land Is It Anyway? A Manual for Decolonization* (Federation of Post-Secondary Educators of British Columbia, 2018), 74.

26 Glen Sean Coulthard, *Red Skin, White Masks: Rejecting the Colonial Politics of Recognition* (Minneapolis: University of Minnesota Press, 2014), 22.

27 Cheryl Bartlett, Murdena Marshall, and Albert Marshall, "Two-Eyed Seeing and Other Lessons Learned within a Co-learning Journey of Bringing Together Indigenous and Mainstream Knowledges and Ways of Knowing," *Journal of Environmental Studies and Sciences* 2, no. 4 (2012): 331–40. The authors note, "we believe that if participants do not or cannot acknowledge that they

need each other and that they need to engage in meaningful co-learning, then an attempt to weave Indigenous Knowledge and mainstream knowledges and ways of knowing is destined to evolve into mere show, the only question being how long that might take." Ibid., 334.

28 Ibid., 331.

29 Ibid., 334.

30 Ibid.

31 Joe Kincheloe and Shirley R. Steinberg, "Indigenous Knowledges in Education: Complexities, Dangers, and Profound Benefits," in Norman K. Denzin, Yvonna S. Lincoln, and Linda Tuhiwai Smith, eds, *Handbook of Critical and Indigenous Methodologies* (Thousand Oaks, CA: SAGE Publications Ltd., 2008), 144, 154.

32 Theodore Michael Christou, "Educational History and the Public Good," *Antistasis* no. 1 (2010): 6.

33 Ibid.

34 Ibid.

35 Luella Bruce Creighton, *Canada: The Struggle for Empire* (Toronto: J.M. Dent & Sons, 1960), 5.

36 Ibid.

37 Ibid., 23.

38 Truth and Reconciliation Commission, *The History, Part 2 1940 to 2000*.

39 Graham Buckingham, *Thompson, a City and Its People* (Thompson, MB: Thompson Historical Society, 1988), cover jacket leaflet.

40 Ibid., 121.

41 Ibid., 16.

42 Ibid., 136.

43 Ibid., cover jacket leaflet.

44 John M. Bumsted and Michael C. Bumsted, *A History of the Canadian Peoples* (Toronto: Oxford University Press, 2016), 37.

45 Ibid.

46 Christou, "Educational History," 7.

47 Ibid.

48 Alison Norman, "'Teachers amongst Their Own People:' Kanyen'kehá: ka (Mohawk) Women Teachers in Nineteenth-Century Tyendinaga and Grand River, Ontario," *Historical Studies in Education/Revue d'histoire de l'éducation* 29, no. 1 (2017): 34.

49 Truth and Reconciliation Commission, *The Survivors Speak: A Report of the Truth and Reconciliation Commission of Canada* (Winnipeg: Truth and Reconciliation Commission of Canada, 2015), xii.

50 Ibid., contents.

51 Ibid., 103.

52 Ibid., 131.

53 A.C. Grayling, *The Choice of Hercules: Pleasure, Duty, and the Good Life in the 21st Century* (London, UK: Weidenfeld & Nicolson, 2007), 55.

54 After 1945, St Peter Claver's Indian Residential School was known as Garnier Residential School.

55 Basil H. Johnston, *Indian School Days* (Norman: University of Oklahoma Press, 1995), 11.

56 Ibid., 7.

57 Ibid., 138.

58 Rita Joe, and Lynn Henry, *Song of Rita Joe: Autobiography of a Mi'kmaq Poet* (Lincoln: University of Nebraska Press, 1996), 50.

59 Ibid., 14.

60 Theodore Fontaine, *Broken Circle: The Dark Legacy of Indian Residential Schools: A Memoir* (Vancouver: Heritage House Publishing Co., 2010), 123.

61 Ibid., 205.

62 Bev Sellars, *They Called Me Number One* (Vancouver: Talonbooks, 2013), 23.

63 Ibid., 165.

64 Ibid., 169.

65 Ibid., 191.

66 Joseph Auguste Merasty and David Carpenter, *The Education of Augie Merasty: A Residential School Memoir* (University of Regina Press, 2017), 38, 42.

67 Edmund Metatawabin and Alexandra Shimo, *Up Ghost River: A Chief's Journey through the Turbulent Waters of Native History* (Toronto: Vintage Canada, 2015), 286.

68 Canada, Parliament, Standing Committee of Aboriginal Affairs and Northern Development. *Evidence.* 1st Sess, 38th Parliament, 17 February 2005. https://www.ourcommons.ca/DocumentViewer/en/38-1/AANO/meeting-19/evidence.

69 Ibid. The Alternative Dispute Resolution (ADR) was the original compensation plan for the Indian Residential School Settlement that Spirit Wind contested. See note 28 of chapter "Spirit Wind," in this volume.

70 Metatawabin and Shimo, *Up Ghost River*, 289.

71 In November 2019, Raymond became the spokesperson of 680 Indian day schools that were left out of previous class action lawsuits. Cullen Crozier, "'You'll Never Have Reconciliation until You Deal with Us': Excluded Survivors Push for Recognition," APTN News, 3 December 2019. https://aptnnews.ca/2019/11/29/youll-never-have-reconciliation-until-you-deal-with-us-excluded-survivors-push-for-recognition/.

72 Søren Kierkegaard, *Fear and Trembling*, trans. A. Hannay (New York: Penguin, 2005), 52.

73 Bartlett, Marshall, and Marshall, "Two-eyed Seeing and Other Lessons Learned," 332.

74 Ibid., 336.

75 Cheryle Partridge, "Residential Schools: The Intergenerational Impacts on Aboriginal Peoples," *Native Social Work Journal: Promising Practices in Mental*

Health: Emerging Paradigms for Aboriginal Social Work Practices 7 (November 2010): 33–62 at 43.

76 Partridge uses the following quote at the beginning and end of "Residential Schools: The Intergenerational Impacts on Aboriginal Peoples," 34 and 59: "What people didn't understand is that those boarding (residential) school terrorists thought that it (culture) could disappear in a generation, and they would have white thinking children. They couldn't erase it, and therein lies the hope. Right there. And when that spirit is reawakened it is more powerful than anything that I have ever met in my whole life. I am impressed with the strength of culture. Even though the missionaries tried, the boarding (residential) schools tried, all the well-intentioned little white people tried ... But something hasn't died."

77 Canada, Parliament, Standing Committee of Aboriginal Affairs and Northern Development. *Evidence.* 1st Sess, 38th Parliament, 17 February 2005.

INDEX

A page reference in italics indicates a photograph. The abbreviation "RM" has been used for "Raymond Mason" in subheadings.